THE STORY OF MY HEART. MY AUTOBIOGRAPHY

Published @ 2017 Trieste Publishing Pty Ltd

ISBN 9780649105304

The story of my heart. My autobiography by Richard Jefferies

Edited by Trieste Publishing Pty Ltd.
Cover @ 2017

www.triestepublishing.com

RICHARD JEFFERIES

THE STORY OF MY HEART. MY AUTOBIOGRAPHY

Trieste

THE
STORY OF MY HEART

THE STORY OF
MY HEART

MY AUTOBIOGRAPHY

BY

RICHARD JEFFERIES

AUTHOR OF "THE GAMEKEEPER AT HOME,"
"WILD LIFE IN A SOUTHERN COUNTY,"
ETC.

WITH FRONTISPIECE

NEW IMPRESSION

LONGMANS, GREEN AND CO.

39 PATERNOSTER ROW, LONDON, E.C. 4
55 FIFTH AVENUE, NEW YORK
BOMBAY, CALCUTTA AND MADRAS

1922

BIBLIOGRAPHICAL NOTE

First printed September 1883.

SILVER LIBRARY EDITION, *June* 1891.

Reprinted August 1891 ; *July* 1894 ; *November* 1896 ;
    December 1898 ; *October* 1901 ; *August* 1904 ;
    April 1906 ; *August* 1910.

POCKET EDITION, *February* 1907.

Reprinted April 1908 ; *March* 1911 ; *October* 1913 ;
    July 1917 ; *January* 1920 ; *February* 1922.

PREFACE

THE title of this book is "The Story of my
Heart: my Autobiography," but it is not an
autobiography in the ordinary sense of the
word. In contains no history of the events
of Richard Jefferies' life. It is in no way
concerned with his birth or his marriage,
his actions or his fortunes. All that is
known of these has been told in "The
Eulogy of Richard Jefferies," by Walter
Besant. *Sunt lachrymæ rerum*, as the ancient poet sang, and for those who have
tears to shed, what story is there more
sure to draw them than that tale of heroic
struggle against the agony of disease, of

genius unappreciated until it was too late, of lofty aspirations and noble thought cut short all too soon?

But none of these things are dwelt on in "The Story of my Heart." Surely it is one of the most singular books that man of genius ever wrote. It is well described by its title. It is an outpouring of Jefferies' innermost soul. Like many another, he found himself at odds with the world. He saw the beauty of the land, the grandeur of the sea, the interest of life—above all of human life— but he was not satisfied. He longed for more beauty, a fuller grandeur, a deeper interest. This feeling completely mastered him, and in "The Story of my Heart" he poured out with what strength and what skill he possessed the intensity of his long- ing. In republishing such a book it will not be thought out of place to gather together such few scraps of his writing as remain

which seem to throw light on its genesis
and its meaning.

On June 22, 1883, Jefferies wrote as
follows :—

SAVERNAKE, LORNA ROAD,
WEST BRIGHTON,
June 22, 1883.

DEAR SIR,—Thank you for the concession
—I will write the story-sketches and send
them. Mentally, the peasant paper is written: I mean it is composed; the MS. shall
reach you in good time. I have just finished
writing a book about which I have been
meditating seventeen years. I have called it
"The Story of my Heart: an Autobiography,"
and it really is an autobiography, an actual
record of thought. After so much thinking
it only makes one small volume—there are
no words wasted in it. I do not know
whether or no you would care to see the
MS.; if so, I will forward it—I do not

mean for the Magazine. . . . I wonder if you would like my autobiographical confessions.

I remain, faithfully yours,

RICHARD JEFFERIES.

C. J. LONGMAN, Esq.

Jefferies was born in 1848; so that he must have begun thinking about this book when he was eighteen years old.

On June 27, 1883, he wrote:—

I have much pleasure in sending you the MS. by letter post. My book is a real record—unsparing to myself as to all things—absolutely and unflinchingly true.

The book was accepted, and published in due course.

On November 3, 1883, he wrote:—

SAVERNAKE, LORNA ROAD,
WEST BRIGHTON,
November 3, 1883.

DEAR SIR,—Some time since I received a circular asking for an analysis of " My Autobiography " for your " Notes on Books." I have made several futile attempts to concentrate in a short note what I intended to convey in the volume. I find it impossible to do so. I have therefore endeavoured to place myself as it were outside the book, and to look at it as a stranger might. But even to do this I have been obliged to make two short quotations, which I hope is not contrary to your rules. My description of the book is very imperfect; still, it is the best I could do, for, in fact, to describe it properly would need another book. If any of your Readers can write a clearer description for me I should be much obliged.

This explanation is necessary to account

for my delay in furnishing the required note.

I remain, faithfully yours,

RICHARD JEFFERIES.

C. J. LONGMAN, Esq.

The analysis he drew up, which was printed in "Notes on Books" of November 30, 1883, was as follows :—

"This book is a confession. The Author describes the successive stages of emotion and thought through which he passed, till he arrived at the conclusions which are set forth in the latter part of the volume. He claims to have erased from his mind the traditions and learning of the past ages, and to stand face to face with nature and with the unknown. The general aim of the work is to free thought from every trammel, with the view of its entering upon another and larger series of ideas than those which have occupied the brain of man so many centuries. He believes that there is a whole world of ideas outside and beyond those which now exercise us.

"The Author's ideas will be best illustrated by the following extracts :—

"'I remember a cameo of Augustus Cæsar —the head of the emperor is graven in delicate lines, and shows the most exquisite proportions. It is a balanced head, a head adjusted to the calmest intellect. That head when it was living contained a circle of ideas, the largest, the widest, the most profound current in his time. All that philosophy had taught, all that practice, experiment, and empiricism had discovered, was familiar to him. There was no knowledge in the ancient world but what was accessible to the Emperor of Rome. Now at this day there are amongst us heads as finely proportioned as that cut out in the cameo. Though these living men do not possess arbitrary power, the advantages of arbitrary power— as far as knowledge is concerned—are secured to them by education, by the printing-press, and the facilities of our era. It is reasonable to imagine a head of our time filled with the largest, the widest, the most profound ideas current in the age. Augustus Cæsar, however great his intellect, could not in that balanced head have possessed the ideas familiar enough to the living head of this day. As we have a circle of ideas unknown to Augustus Cæsar, so I argue there are whole circles of ideas unknown to us.'

" For himself, for the individual, the Author desires physical perfection—he despises external circumstances.

" ' It is in myself that I desire increase, profit, and exaltation of body, mind, and soul. The surroundings, the clothes, the dwelling, the social status, the circumstances

are to me utterly indifferent. Let the floor
of the room be bare, let the furniture be
a plank table, the bed a mere pallet. Let
the house be plain and simple, but in the
midst of air and light. These are enough
—a cave would be enough; in a warmer
climate the open air would suffice. Let me
be furnished in myself with health, safety,
strength, the perfection of physical existence;
let my mind be furnished with highest
thoughts of soul-life. Let me be in myself
myself fully. The pageantry of power, the
still more foolish pageantry of wealth, the
senseless precedence of place; I fail words
to express my utter contempt for such
pleasure or such ambitions.'

"From all nature—from the universe—
he desires to take its energy, grandeur, and
beauty. He looks forward to the possibility
of ideal man, and adduces reasons for the
possibility of such ideal man living in en-

joyment of his faculties for a great length of time. He is anxious that the culture of the soul should be earnestly carried out, as earnestly as the culture of the body was in ancient Greece, as that of the mind is at the present day. So highly does he place the soul, that if it can but retain its consciousness and attain its desires he thinks it matters not if the entire material world disappears. Yet the work teems with admiration of material beauty. He considers the idea of deity inferior, and believes that there is something higher. He ends as he commences with prayer for the fullest soul-life. The book, in fact, might have been called an Autobiography of a Soul, or of Thought. It is not an autobiography of the petty events of life; from the Author's point of view the soul is the man, and not the clothes he wears."

C. J. LONGMAN.

THE

STORY OF MY HEART

CHAPTER I

THE story of my heart commences seventeen
years ago. In the glow of youth there were
times every now and then when I felt the
necessity of a strong inspiration of soul-
thought. My heart was dusty, parched for
want of the rain of deep feeling; my mind
arid and dry, for there is a dust which settles
on the heart as well as that which falls on a
ledge. It is injurious to the mind as well as
to the body to be always in one place and
always surrounded by the same circumstances.
A species of thick clothing slowly grows about
the mind, the pores are choked, little habits

become a part of existence, and by degrees
the mind is inclosed in a husk. When this
began to form I felt eager to escape from
it, to throw it off like heavy clothing, to
drink deeply once more at the fresh foun-
tains of life. An inspiration—a long deep
breath of the pure air of thought—could
alone give health to the heart.

There was a hill to which I used to resort
at such periods. The labour of walking three
miles to it, all the while gradually ascending,
seemed to clear my blood of the heaviness
accumulated at home. On a warm summer
day the slow continued rise required con-
tinual effort, which carried away the sense
of oppression. The familiar everyday scene
was soon out of sight; I came to other
trees, meadows, and fields; I began to
breathe a new air and to have a fresher
aspiration. I restrained my soul till I
reached the sward of the hill; psyche, the

soul that longed to be loose. I would write psyche always instead of soul to avoid meanings which have become attached to the word soul, but it is awkward to do so. Clumsy indeed are all words the moment the wooden stage of commonplace life is left. I restrained psyche, my soul, till I reached and put my foot on the grass at the beginning of the green hill itself.

Moving up the sweet short turf, at every step my heart seemed to obtain a wider horizon of feeling ; with every inhalation of rich pure air, a deeper desire. The very light of the sun was whiter and more brilliant here. By the time I had reached the summit I had entirely forgotten the petty circumstances and the annoyances of existence. I felt myself, myself. There was an intrenchment on the summit, and going down into the fosse I walked round it slowly to recover breath. On the south-western side there was a spot where the outer bank had partially slipped, leaving a gap. There the view was over a broad plain, beautiful with wheat, and inclosed by a perfect amphitheatre of green hills. Through these hills there was one narrow groove, or pass, southwards, where the white clouds seemed to close in the horizon. Woods hid the scattered hamlets and farmhouses, so that I was quite alone.

I was utterly alone with the sun and the earth. Lying down on the grass, I spoke in my soul to the earth, the sun, the air, and the distant sea far beyond sight. I thought of the earth's firmness—I felt it bear me up; through the grassy couch there came an influence as if I could feel the great earth speaking to me. I thought of the wandering air—its pureness, which is its beauty; the air touched me and gave me something of itself. I spoke to the sea: though so far, in my mind I saw it, green at the rim of the earth and blue in deeper ocean; I desired to have its strength, its mystery and glory. Then I addressed the sun, desiring the soul equivalent of his light and brilliance, his endurance and unwearied race. I turned to the blue heaven over, gazing into its depth, inhaling its exquisite colour and sweetness. The rich blue of the unattainable flower of the sky drew my soul towards it, and there it rested, for pure colour is rest of heart. By all these I prayed; I felt an emotion of the soul beyond all definition; prayer is a puny thing to it, and the word is a rude sign to the feeling, but I know no other.

By the blue heaven, by the rolling sun bursting through untrodden space, a new ocean of ether every day unveiled. By the fresh and wandering air encompassing the world; by the sea sounding on the shore— the green sea white-flecked at the margin and the deep ocean; by the strong earth

under me. Then, returning, I prayed by the
sweet thyme, whose little flowers I touched
with my hand; by the slender grass; by
the crumble of dry chalky earth I took up
and let fall through my fingers. Touching
the crumble of earth, the blade of grass, the
thyme flower, breathing the earth-encircling
air, thinking of the sea and the sky, holding
out my hand for the sunbeams to touch
it, prone on the sward in token of deep
reverence, thus I prayed that I might touch
to the unutterable existence infinitely higher
than deity.

With all the intensity of feeling which
exalted me, all the intense communion I
held with the earth, the sun and sky, the
stars hidden by the light, with the ocean—
in no manner can the thrilling depth of these
feelings be written—with these I prayed, as
if they were the keys of an instrument, of an
organ, with which I swelled forth the notes

of my soul, redoubling my own voice by their power. The great sun burning with light; the strong earth, dear earth; the warm sky; the pure air; the thought of ocean; the inexpressible beauty of all filled me with a rapture, an ecstasy, an inflatus. With this inflatus, too, I prayed. Next to myself I came and recalled myself, my bodily existence. I held out my hand, the sunlight gleamed on the skin and the iridescent nails; I recalled the mystery and beauty of the flesh. I thought of the mind with which I could see the ocean sixty miles distant, and gather to myself its glory. I thought of my inner existence, that consciousness which is called the soul. These, that is, myself—I threw into the balance to weigh the prayer the heavier. My strength of body, mind and soul, I flung into it; I put forth my strength; I wrestled and laboured, and toiled in might of prayer. The prayer, this soul-emotion was in itself—not for an object—it was a passion. I hid my face in the grass, I was wholly prostrated, I lost myself in the wrestle, I was rapt and carried away.

Becoming calmer, I returned to myself and thought, reclining in rapt thought, full of aspiration, steeped to the lips of my soul in desire. I did not then define, or analyse, or understand this. I see now that what I laboured for was soul-life, more soul-nature, to be exalted, to be full of soul-learning. Finally I rose, walked half a mile or so along the summit of the hill eastwards, to soothe myself and come to the common ways of life again. Had any shepherd accidentally seen me lying on the turf, he would only have thought that I was resting a few minutes; I made no outward show. Who could have imagined the whirlwind of passion that was going on within me as I reclined there! I was greatly exhausted when I reached home.

Occasionally I went upon the hill deliberately, deeming it good to do so; then, again, this craving carried me away up there of itself. Though the principal feeling was the same, there were variations in the mode in which it affected me.

Sometimes on lying down on the sward I first looked up at the sky, gazing for a long time till I could see deep into the azure and my eyes were full of the colour; then I turned my face to the grass and thyme, placing my hands at each side of my face so as to shut out everything and hide myself. Having drunk deeply of the heaven above and felt the most glorious beauty of the day, and remembering the old, old sea, which (as it seemed to me) was but just yonder at the edge, I now became lost, and absorbed into the being or existence of the universe. I felt down deep into the earth under, and high above into the sky, and farther still to the sun and stars. Still farther beyond the stars into the hollow of space, and losing thus my separateness of being came to seem like a part of the whole. Then I whispered to the earth beneath, through the grass and thyme, down into the depth of its ear, and again up to the starry space hid behind the blue of day. Travelling in an instant across the distant sea, I saw as if with actual vision the palms and cocoanut trees, the bamboos of India, and the cedars of the extreme south. Like a lake with islands the ocean lay before me, as clear and vivid as the plain beneath in the midst of the amphitheatre of hills.

With the glory of the great sea, I said; with the firm, solid, and sustaining earth; the depth, distance, and expanse of ether; the age, tamelessness, and ceaseless motion of the ocean; the stars, and the unknown in space; by all those things which are most powerful known to me, and by those which exist, but of which I have no idea whatever, I pray. Further, by my own soul, that secret existence which above all other things bears the nearest resemblance to the ideal of spirit, infinitely nearer than earth, sun, or star. Speaking by an inclination towards, not in words, my soul prays that I may have something from each of these, that I may gather a flower from them, that I may have in myself the secret and meaning of the earth, the golden sun, the light, the foam-flecked sea. Let my soul become enlarged; I am not enough; I am little and contemptible. I desire a greatness of soul, an irradiance of mind, a deeper insight, a broader hope. Give me power of soul, so that I may actually effect by its will that which I strive for.

In winter, though I could not then rest on the grass, or stay long enough to form any definite expression, I still went up to the hill once now and then, for it seemed that to merely visit the spot repeated all that I had previously said. But it was not only then.

In summer I went out into the fields, and let my soul inspire these thoughts under the trees, standing against the trunk, or looking up through the branches at the sky. If trees could speak, hundreds of them would say that I had had these soul-emotions under them. Leaning against the oak's massive trunk, and feeling the rough bark and the lichen at my back, looking southwards over the grassy fields, cowslip-yellow, at the woods on the slope, I thought my desire of deeper soul-life. Or under the green firs, looking upwards, the sky was more deeply blue at their tops; then the brake fern was unrolling, the doves cooing, the thickets astir, the late ash-leaves coming forth. Under the shapely rounded elms, by the hawthorn bushes and hazel, everywhere the same deep desire for the soul-nature; to have from all green things and from the sunlight the inner meaning which was not known to them, that I might be full of light as the woods of the sun's rays. Just to touch the lichened bark of a tree, or the end of a spray projecting over the path as I walked, seemed to repeat the same prayer in me.

The long-lived summer days dried and warmed the turf in the meadows. I used to lie down in solitary corners at full length on my back, so as to feel the embrace of the earth. The grass stood high above me, and the shadows of the tree-branches danced on my face. I looked up at the sky, with half-closed eyes to bear the dazzling light. Bees buzzed over me, sometimes a butterfly passed, there was a hum in the air, greenfinches sang in the hedge. Gradually entering into the intense life of the summer days—a life which burned around as if every grass blade and leaf were a torch—I came to feel the long-drawn life of the earth back into the dimmest past, while the sun of the moment was warm on me. Sesostris on the most ancient sands of the south, in ancient, ancient days, was conscious of himself and of the sun. This sunlight linked me through the ages to that past consciousness. From all the ages my soul desired to take that soul-life which had flowed through them as the sunbeams had continually poured on earth. As the hot sands take up the heat, so would I take up that soul-energy. Dreamy in appearance, I was breathing full of existence; I was aware of the grass blades, the flowers, the leaves on hawthorn and tree. I seemed to live more largely through them, as if each were a pore through which I drank. The grass-hoppers called and leaped, the greenfinches sang, the blackbirds happily fluted, all the air hummed with life. I was plunged deep in existence, and with all that existence I prayed.

Through every grass blade in the thousand, thousand grasses; through the million leaves, veined and edge - cut, on bush and tree; through the song - notes and the marked feathers of the birds; through the insects' hum and the colour of the butterflies; through the soft warm air, the flecks of clouds dissolving—I used them all for prayer. With all the energy the sunbeams had poured unwearied on the earth since Sesostris was conscious of them on the ancient sands; with all the life that had been lived by vigorous man and beauteous woman since first in dearest Greece the dream of the gods was woven; with all the soul-life that had flowed a long stream down to me, I prayed that I might have a soul more than equal to, far beyond my conception of, these things of the past, the present, and the fulness of all life. Not only equal to these, but beyond, higher, and more powerful than I could imagine. That I might take from all their energy, grandeur, and beauty, and gather it into me. That my soul might be more than the cosmos of life.

I prayed with the glowing clouds of sunset and the soft light of the first star coming through the violet sky. At night with the stars, according to the season : now with the Pleiades, now with the Swan or burning Sirius, and broad Orion's whole constellation, red Aldebaran, Arcturus, and the Northern Crown; with the morning star, the light-bringer, once now and then when I saw it, a white-gold ball in the violet-purple sky, or framed about with pale summer vapour floating away as red streaks shot horizontally in the east. A diffused saffron ascended into the luminous upper azure. The disk of the sun rose over the hill, fluctuating with throbs of light; his chest heaved in fervour of brilliance. All the glory of the sunrise filled me with broader and furnace-like vehemence of prayer. That I might have the deepest of soul-life, the deepest of all, deeper far than all this greatness of the visible universe and even of the invisible; that I might have a fulness of soul till now unknown, and utterly beyond my own conception.

.In the deepest darkness of the night the same thought rose in my mind as in the bright light of noontide. What is there which I have not used to strengthen the same emotion?

B

CHAPTER II

SOMETIMES I went to a deep, narrow valley
in the hills, silent and solitary. The sky
crossed from side to side, like a roof supported
on two walls of green. Sparrows chirped in
the wheat at the verge above, their calls falling like the twittering of swallows from the
air. There was no other sound. The short
grass was dried grey as it grew by the heat;
the sun hung over the narrow vale as if it
had been put there by hand. Burning, burning, the sun glowed on the sward at the foot
of the slope where these thoughts burned
into me. How many, many years, how
many cycles of years, how many bundles of
cycles of years, had the sun glowed down
thus on that hollow? Since it was formed

how long? Since it was worn and shaped, groove-like, in the flanks of the hills by mighty forces which had ebbed. Alone with the sun which glowed on the work when it was done, I saw back through space to the old time of tree-ferns, of the lizard flying through the air, the lizard-dragon wallowing in sea foam, the mountainous creatures, twice-elephantine, feeding on land; all the crooked sequence of life. The dragon-fly which passed me traced a continuous descent from the fly marked on stone in those days. The immense time lifted me like a wave rolling under a boat; my mind seemed to raise itself as the swell of the cycles came; it felt strong with the power of the ages. With all that time and power I prayed: that I might have in my soul the intellectual part of it; the idea, the thought. Like a shuttle the mind shot to and fro the past and the present, in an instant.

Full to the brim of the wondrous past, I felt the wondrous present. For the day—the very moment I breathed, that second of time then in the valley, was as marvellous, as grand, as all that had gone before. Now, this moment was the wonder and the glory. Now, this moment was exceedingly wonderful. Now, this moment give me all the thought, all the idea, all the soul expressed in the cosmos around me. Give me still more, for the interminable universe, past and present, is but earth; give me the unknown soul, wholly apart from it, the soul of which I know only that when I touch the ground, when the sunlight touches my hand, it is not there. Therefore the heart looks into space to be away from earth. With all the cycles, and the sunlight streaming through them, with all that is meant by the present, I thought in the deep vale and prayed.

There was a secluded spring to which I
sometimes went to drink the pure water,
lifting it in the hollow of my hand. Drinking
the lucid water, clear as light itself in solution, I absorbed the beauty and purity of it.
I drank the thought of the element; I desired
soul-nature pure and limpid. When I saw
the sparkling dew on the grass—a rainbow
broken into drops—it called up the same
thought-prayer. The stormy wind whose
sudden twists laid the trees on the ground
woke the same feeling; my heart shouted
with it. The soft summer air which entered
when I opened my window in the morning
breathed the same sweet desire. At night,
before sleeping, I always looked out at the
shadowy trees, the hills looming indistinctly
in the dark, a star seen between the drifting
clouds; prayer of soul-life always. I chose
the highest room, bare and gaunt, because
as I sat at work I could look out and see

more of the wide earth, more of. the dome of the sky, and could think my desire through these. When the crescent of the new moon shone, all the old thoughts were renewed.

All the succeeding incidents of the year repeated my prayer as I noted them. The first green leaf on the hawthorn, the first spike of meadow grass, the first song of the nightingale, the green ear of wheat. I spoke it with the ear of wheat as the sun tinted it golden; with the whitening barley; again with the red gold spots of autumn on the beech, the buff oak leaves, and the gossamer dew-weighted. All the larks over the green corn sang it for me, all the dear swallows; the green leaves rustled it; the green brook-flags waved it; the swallows took it with them to repeat it for me in distant lands. By the running brook I meditated it; a flash of sunlight here in the curve, a flicker yonder on the ripples, the birds bathing in the sandy shallow, the rush of falling water. As the brook ran winding through the meadow, so one thought ran winding through my days.

The sciences I studied never checked it for a moment; nor did the books of old philosophy. The sun was stronger than science; the hills more than philosophy. Twice circumstances gave me a brief view of the sea; then the passion rose tumultuous as the waves. It was very bitter to me to leave the sea.

Sometimes I spent the whole day walking over the hills searching for it; as if the labour of walking would force it from the ground. I remained in the woods for hours, among the ash sprays and the fluttering of the ring-doves at their nests, the scent of pines here and there, dreaming my prayer.

My work was most uncongenial and use-less, but even then sometimes a gleam of sunlight on the wall, the buzz of a bee at the window, would bring the thought to me. Only to make me miserable, for it was a waste of golden time while the rich sunlight streamed on hill and plain. There was a wrenching of the mind, a straining of the mental sinews; I was forced to do this, my mind was yonder. Weariness, exhaustion, nerve-illness often ensued. The insults which are showered on poverty, long struggle of labour, the heavy pressure of circumstances, the unhappiness, only stayed the expression of the feeling. It was always there. Often in the streets of London, as the red sunset flamed over the houses, the old thought, the old prayer, came.

Not only in grassy fields with green leaf and running brook did this constant desire find renewal. More deeply still with living human beauty; the perfection of form, the simple fact of form, ravished and always will

ravish me away. In this lies the outcome
and end of all the loveliness of sunshine and
green leaf, of flowers, pure water, and sweet
air. This is embodiment and highest expression; the scattered, uncertain, and designless loveliness of tree and sunlight
brought to shape. Through this beauty I
prayed deepest and longest, and down to this
hour. The shape—the divine idea of that
shape—the swelling muscle or the dreamy
limb, strong sinew or curve of bust, Aphrodite or Hercules, it is the same. That I may
have the soul-life, the soul-nature, let divine
beauty bring to me divine soul. Swart
Nubian, white Greek, delicate Italian, massive Scandinavian, in all the exquisite
pleasure the form gave, and gives, to me
immediately becomes intense prayer.

If I could have been in physical shape
like these, how despicable in comparison I
am; to be shapely of form is so infinitely

beyond wealth, power, fame, all that ambition can give, that these are dust before it. Unless of the human form, no pictures hold me; the rest are flat surfaces. So, too, with the other arts, they are dead; the potters, the architects, meaningless, stony, and some repellent, like the cold touch of porcelain. No prayer with these. Only the human form in art could raise it, and most in statuary. I have seen so little good statuary, it is a regret to me; still, that I have is beyond all other art. Fragments here, a bust yonder, the broken pieces brought from Greece, copies, plaster casts, a memory of an Aphrodite, of a Persephone, of an Apollo, that is all; but even drawings of statuary will raise the prayer. These statues were like myself full of a thought, for ever about to burst forth as a bud, yet silent in the same attitude. Give me to live the soul-life they express. The smallest fragment of marble carved in the shape of the human arm will wake the desire I felt in my hill-prayer.

Time went on; good fortune and success never for an instant deceived me that they were in themselves to be sought; only my soul-thought was worthy. Further years bringing much suffering, grinding the very life out; new troubles, renewed insults, loss of what hard labour had earned, the bitter question: Is it not better to leap into the sea? These, too, have made no impression; constant still to the former prayer my mind endures. It was my chief regret that I had not endeavoured to write these things, to give expression to this passion. I am now trying, but I see that I shall only in part succeed.

The same prayer comes to me at this very hour. It is now less solely associated with the sun and sea, hills, woods, or beauteous human shape. It is always within.

It requires no waking; no renewal; it is always with me. I am it; the fact of my existence expresses it.

After a long interval I came to the hills again, this time by the coast. I found a deep hollow on the side of a great hill, a green concave opening to the sea, where I could rest and think in perfect quiet. Behind me were furze bushes dried by the heat; immediately in front dropped the steep descent of the bowl-like hollow which received and brought up to me the faint sound of the summer waves. Yonder lay the immense plain of sea, the palest green under the continued sunshine, as though the heat had evaporated the colour from it; there was no distinct horizon, a heat-mist inclosed it and looked farther away than the horizon would have done. Silence and sunshine, sea and hill gradually brought my mind into the condition of intense prayer. Day after day, for hours at a time, I came there, my soul-desire always the same. Presently I began to consider how I could put a part of that prayer into form, giving it an object. Could I bring it into such a shape as would admit of actually working upon the lines it indicated for any good?

One evening, when the bright white star in Lyra was shining almost at the zenith over me, and the deep concave was the more profound in the dusk, I formulated it into three divisions. First, I desired that I might do or find something to exalt the soul, something to enable it to live its own life, a more powerful existence now. Secondly, I desired to be able to do something for the flesh, to make a discovery or perfect a method by which the fleshly body might enjoy more pleasure, longer life, and suffer less pain. Thirdly, to construct a more flexible engine with which to carry into execution the design of the will. I called this the Lyra prayer, to distinguish it from the far deeper emotion in which the soul was alone concerned.

Of the three divisions, the last was of so little importance that it scarcely deserved to be named in conjunction with the others. Mechanism increases convenience—in no degree does it confer physical or moral perfection. The rudimentary engines employed thousands of years ago in raising buildings were in that respect equal to the complicated machines of the present day. Control of iror and steel has not altered or improved the bodily man. I even debated some time whether such a third division should be included at all. Our bodies are now conveyed all round the world with ease, but obtain no advantage. As they start so they return. The most perfect human families of ancient times were almost stationary, as those of Greece. Perfection of form was found in

Sparta; how small a spot compared to those continents over which we are now taken so quickly! Such perfection of form might perhaps again dwell, contented and complete in itself, on such a strip of land as I could see between me and the sand of the sea. Again, a watch keeping correct time is no guarantee that the bearer shall not suffer pain. The owner of the watch may be soulless, without mind-fire, a mere creature. No benefit to the heart or to the body accrues from the most accurate mechanism. Hence I debated whether the third division should be included. But I reflected that time cannot be put back on the dial, we cannot return to Sparta; there is an existent state of things, and existent multitudes; and possibly a more powerful engine, flexible to the will, might give them that freedom which is the one, and the one only, political or social idea I possess. For liberty, therefore, let it be included.

For the flesh, this arm of mine, the limbs
of others gracefully moving, let me find
something that will give them greater perfection. That the bones may be firmer,
somewhat larger if that would be an advantage, certainly stronger, that the cartilage
and sinews may be more enduring, and the
muscles more powerful, something after the
manner of those ideal limbs and muscles
sculptured of old, these in the flesh and real.
That the organs of the body may be stronger
in their action, perfect, and lasting. That
the exterior flesh may be yet more beautiful;
that the shape may be finer, and the motions
graceful. These are the soberest words I
can find, purposely chosen; for I am so rapt
in the beauty of the human form, and so
earnestly, so inexpressibly, prayerful to see
that form perfect, that my full thought is
not to be written. Unable to express it fully,
I have considered it best to put it in the

simplest manner of words. I believe in the human form; let me find something, some method, by which that form may achieve the utmost beauty. Its beauty is like an arrow, which may be shot any distance according to the strength of the bow. So the idea expressed in the human shape is capable of indefinite expansion and elevation of beauty.

Of the mind, the inner consciousness, the soul, my prayer desired that I might discover a mode of life for it, so that it might not only conceive of such a life, but actually enjoy it on the earth. I wished to search out a new and higher set of ideas on which the mind should work. The simile of a new book of the soul is the nearest to convey the meaning —a book drawn from the present and future, not the past. Instead of a set of ideas based on tradition, let me give the mind a new thought drawn straight from the wondrous present, direct this very hour. Next, to furnish the soul with the means of executing its will, of carrying thought into action. In other words, for the soul to become a power. These three formed the Lyra prayer, of which the two first are immeasurably the more important.   I believe in the human being, mind and flesh; form and soul.

It happened just afterwards that I went to Pevensey, and immediately the ancient wall swept my mind back seventeen hundred years to the eagle, the pilum, and the short sword. The grey stones, the thin red bricks laid by those whose eyes had seen Cæsar's Rome, lifted me out of the grasp of house-life, of modern civilisation, of those minutiæ which occupy the moment. The grey stone made me feel as if I had existed from then till now, so strongly did I enter into and see my own life as if reflected. My own exist-ence was focussed back on me; I saw its joy, its unhappiness, its birth, its death, its possibilities among the infinite, above all its yearning Question. Why? Seeing it thus clearly, and lifted out of the moment by the force of seventeen centuries, I recognised the full mystery and the depths of things in the roots of the dry grass on the wall, in the green sea flowing near. Is there anything I can do? The mystery and the possibilities are not in the roots of the grass, nor is the depth of things in the sea; they are in my existence, in my soul. The marvel of existence, almost the terror of it, was flung on me with crushing force by the sea, the sun shining, the distant hills. With all their ponderous weight they made me feel myself: all the time, all the centuries made me feel myself this moment a hundred-fold. I determined that I would endeavour to write what I had so long thought of, and the same evening put down one sentence. There the sentence remained two years. I tried to carry it on ; I hesitated because I could not express it : nor can I now, though in desperation I am throwing these rude stones of thought together, rude as those of the ancient wall.

CHAPTER III

THERE were grass-grown tumuli on the hills
to which of old I used to walk, sit down at
the foot of one of them, and think. Some
warrior had been interred there in the ante-
historic times. The sun of the summer morning shone on the dome of sward, and the air
came softly up from the wheat below, the tips
of the grasses swayed as it passed sighing
faintly, it ceased, and the bees hummed by
to the thyme and heathbells. I became absorbed in the glory of the day, the sunshine,
the sweet air, the yellowing corn turning
from its sappy green to summer's noon of
gold, the lark's song like a waterfall in the
sky. I felt at that moment that I was
like the spirit of the man whose body was

37

interred in the tumulus; I could understand and feel his existence the same as my own. He was as real to me two thousand years after interment as those I had seen in the body. The abstract personality of the dead seemed as existent as thought. As my thought could slip back the twenty centuries in a moment to the forest-days when he hurled the spear, or shot with the bow, hunting the deer, and could return again as swiftly to this moment, so his spirit could endure from then till now, and the time was nothing.

Two thousand years being a second to the soul could not cause its extinction. It was no longer to the soul than my thought occupied to me. Recognising my own inner consciousness, the psyche, so clearly, death did not seem to me to affect the personality. In dissolution there was no bridgeless chasm, no unfathomable gulf of separation; the spirit did not immediately become inaccessible, leaping at a bound to an immeasurable distance. Look at another person while living; the soul is not visible, only the body which it animates. Therefore, merely because after death the soul is not visible is no demonstration that it does not still live. The condition of being unseen is the same condition which occurs while the body is living, so that intrinsically there is nothing exceptionable, or supernatural, in the life of the soul after death. Resting by the tumulus, the spirit of the man who had been interred there was to me really alive, and very close. This was quite natural, as natural and simple as the grass waving in the wind, the bees humming, and the larks' songs. Only by the strongest effort of the mind could I understand the idea of extinction; that was supernatural, requiring a miracle; the immortality of the soul natural, like earth.

Listening to the sighing of the grass I felt immortality as I felt the beauty of the summer morning, and I thought beyond immortality, of other conditions, more beautiful than existence, higher than immortality.

That there is no knowing, in the sense of written reasons, whether the soul lives on or not, I am fully aware. I do not hope or fear. At least while I am living I have enjoyed the idea of immortality, and the idea of my own soul. If then, after death, I am resolved without exception into earth, air, and water, and the spirit goes out like a flame, still I shall have had the glory of that thought.

It happened once that a man was drowned while bathing, and his body was placed in an outhouse near the garden. I passed the outhouse continually, sometimes on purpose to think about it, and it always seemed to me that the man was still living. Separation is not to be comprehended ; the spirit of the man did not appear to have gone to an inconceivable distance. As my thought flashes itself back through the centuries to the luxury of Canopus, and can see the gilded couches of a city extinct, so it slips through the future, and immeasurable time in front is no boundary to it. Certainly the man was not dead to me.

Sweetly the summer air came up to the tumulus, the grass sighed softly, the butterflies went by, sometimes alighting on the green dome. Two thousand years ! Summer after summer the blue butterflies had visited the mound, the thyme had flowered, the wind sighed in the grass. The azure morning had spread its arms over the low tomb ; and full glowing noon burned on it ; the purple of sunset rosied the sward. Stars, ruddy in the vapour of the southern horizon, beamed at midnight through the mystic summer night, which is dusky and yet full of light. White mists swept up and hid it; dews rested on the turf; tender harebells drooped; the wings of the finches fanned the air—finches whose colours faded from the wings how many centuries ago! Brown autumn dwelt in the woods beneath; the rime of winter whitened the beech clump on the ridge; again the buds came on the wind-blown hawthorn bushes, and in the evening the broad con-stellation of Orion covered the east. Two thousand times! Two thousand times the woods grew green, and ring-doves built their nests. Day and night for two thousand years—light and shadow sweeping over the mound—two thousand years of labour by day and slumber by night. Mystery gleaming in the stars, pouring down in the sunshine, speaking in the night, the wonder of the sun and of far space, for twenty centuries round about this low and green-grown dome. Yet all that mystery and wonder is as nothing to the Thought that lies therein, to the spirit that I feel so close.

Realising that spirit, recognising my own inner consciousness, the psyche, so clearly, I cannot understand time. It is eternity now. I am in the midst of it. It is about me in the sunshine; I am in it, as the butterfly floats in the light-laden air. Nothing has to come; it is now. Now is eternity; now is the immortal life. Here this moment, by this tumulus, on earth, now; I exist in it. The years, the centuries, the cycles are absolutely nothing; it is only a moment since this tumulus was raised; in a thousand years more it will still be only a moment. To the soul there is no past and no future; all is and will be ever, in now. For artificial purposes time is mutually agreed on, but there is really no such thing. The shadow goes on upon the dial, the index moves round upon the clock, and what is the difference? None whatever. If the clock had never been set going, what would have been the difference? There may be time for the clock, the clock may make time for itself; there is none for me.

I dip my hand in the brook and feel the stream; in an instant the particles of water which first touched me have floated yards down the current, my hand remains there. I take my hand away, and the flow—the time—of the brook does not exist to me. The great clock of the firmament, the sun and the stars, the crescent moon, the earth circling two thousand times, is no more to me than the flow of the brook when my hand is withdrawn; my soul has never been, and never can be, dipped in time. Time has never existed, and never will; it is a purely artificial arrangement. It is eternity now, it always was eternity, and always will be. By no possible means could I get into time if I tried. I am in eternity now and must there remain. Haste not, be at rest, this Now is eternity. Because the idea of time has left my mind—if ever it had any hold on it—to me the man interred in the tumulus is living now as I live. We are both in eternity.

There is no separation—no past; eternity, the Now, is continuous. When all the stars have revolved they only produce Now again. The continuity of Now is for ever. So that it appears to me purely natural, and not super-natural, that the soul whose temporary frame was interred in this mound should be existing as I sit on the sward. How infinitely deeper is thought than the million miles of the firma-ment! The wonder is here, not there; now, not to be, now always. Things that have been miscalled supernatural appear to me simple, more natural than nature, than earth, than sea, or sun. It is beyond telling more natural that I should have a soul than not, that there should be immortality; I think there is much more than immortality. It is matter which is the supernatural, and difficult of understanding. Why this clod of earth I hold in my hand? Why this water which drops sparkling from my fingers dipped in the brook? Why are they at all? When? How? What for? Matter is beyond understanding, mysterious, impenetrable; I touch it easily, comprehend it, no. Soul, mind—the thought, the idea—is easily understood, it understands itself and is conscious.

The supernatural miscalled, the natural in truth, is the real. To me everything is supernatural. How strange that condition of mind which cannot accept anything but the earth, the sea, the tangible universe! Without the misnamed supernatural these to

me seem incomplete, unfinished. Without
soul all these are dead. Except when I walk
by the sea, and my soul is by it, the sea
is dead. Those seas by which no man has
stood—by which no soul has been—whether
on earth or the planets, are dead. No matter
how majestic the planet rolls in space, unless
a soul be there it is dead. As I move about
in the sunshine I feel in the midst of the
supernatural: in the midst of immortal things.
It is impossible to wrest the mind down to
the same laws that rule pieces of timber, water,
or earth. They do not control the soul, however rigidly they may bind matter. So full
am I always of a sense of the immortality
now at this moment round about me, that
it would not surprise me in the least if a
circumstance outside physical experience occurred. It would seem to me quite natural.
Give the soul the power it conceives, and
there would be nothing wonderful in it.

I can see nothing astonishing in what are called miracles. Only those who are mesmerised by matter can find a difficulty in such events. I am aware that the evidence for miracles is logically and historically untrustworthy; I am not defending recorded miracles. My point is that in principle I see no reason at all why they should not take place this day. I do not even say that there are or ever have been miracles, but I maintain that they would be perfectly natural. The wonder rather is that they do not happen frequently. Consider the limitless conceptions of the soul: let it possess but the power to realise those conceptions for one hour, and how little, how trifling would be the helping of the injured or the sick to regain health and happiness—merely to think it. A soul-work would require but a thought. Soul-work is an expression better suited to my meaning than "miracle," a term like others into which a special sense has been infused.

When I consider that I dwell this moment in the eternal Now that has ever been and will be, that I am in the midst of immortal things this moment, that there probably are Souls as infinitely superior to mine as mine to a piece of timber, what then, pray, is a " miracle " ? As commonly understood, a " miracle " is a mere nothing. I can conceive soul-works done by simple will or thought a thousand times greater. I marvel that they do not happen this moment. The air, the sunlight, the night, all that surrounds me seems crowded with inexpressible powers, with the influence of Souls, or existences, so that I walk in the midst of immortal things. I myself am a living witness of it. Sometimes I have concentrated myself, and driven away by continued will all sense of outward appearances, looking straight with the full power of my mind inwards on myself. I find " I " am there; an " I " I do not wholly understand, or know—something is there distinct from earth and timber, from flesh and bones. Recognising it, I feel on the margin of a life unknown, very near, almost touching it: on the verge of powers which if I could grasp would give me an immense breadth of existence, an ability to execute what I now only conceive; most probably of far more than that. To see that " I " is to know that I am surrounded with immortal things. If, when I die, that " I " also dies, and becomes extinct, still even then I have had the exaltation of these ideas.

How many words it has taken to describe so briefly the feelings and the thoughts that came to me by the tumulus; thoughts that swept past and were gone, and were succeeded by others while yet the shadow of the mound had not moved from one thyme-flower to another, not the breadth of a grass blade. Softly breathed the sweet south wind, gently the yellow corn waved beneath; the ancient, ancient sun shone on the fresh grass and the flower, my heart opened wide as the broad, broad earth. I spread my arms out, laying them on the sward, seizing the grass, to take the fulness of the days. Could I have my own way after death I would be burned on a pyre of pine-wood, open to the air, and placed on the summit of the hills. Then let my ashes be scattered abroad—not collected in an urn—freely sown wide and broadcast. That is the natural interment of man—of man whose Thought at least has been among the immortals; interment in the elements. Burial is not enough, it does not give sufficient solution into the elements speedily; a furnace is confined. The high open air of the topmost hill, there let the tawny flame lick up the fragment called the body; there cast the ashes into the space it longed for while living. Such a luxury of interment is only for the wealthy; I fear I shall not be able to afford it. Else the smoke of my resolution into the elements should certainly arise in time on the hill-top.

The silky grass sighs as the wind comes carrying the blue butterfly more rapidly than his wings. A large humble-bee burrs round the green dome against which I rest; my hands are scented with thyme. The sweetness of the day, the fulness of the earth, the beauteous earth, how shall I say it?

Three things only have been discovered of that which concerns the inner consciousness since before written history began. Three things only in twelve thousand written, or sculptured, years, and in the dumb, dim time before then. Three ideas the Cavemen primeval wrested from the unknown, the night which is round us still in daylight—the existence of the soul, immortality, the deity. These things found, prayer followed as a sequential result. Since then nothing further has been found in all the twelve thousand years, as if men had been satisfied and had found these to suffice. They do not suffice me. I desire to advance further, and to wrest a fourth, and even still more than a fourth, from the darkness of thought. I want more ideas of soul-life. I am certain that there are more yet to be found. A great life—an entire civilisation—lies just outside the pale of common thought. Cities and countries, inhabitants, intelligences, culture—an entire civilisation. Except by illustrations drawn from familiar things, there is no way of indicating a new idea. I do not mean actual cities, actual civilisation. Such life is different from any yet imagined. A nexus of ideas exists of which nothing is known—a vast system of ideas—a cosmos of thought. There is an

Entity, a Soul-Entity, as yet unrecognised. These, rudely expressed, constitute my Fourth Idea. It is beyond, or beside, the three discovered by the Cavemen; it is in addition to the existence of the soul; in addition to immortality; and beyond the idea of the deity. I think there is something more than existence.

There is an immense ocean over which the mind can sail, upon which the vessel of thought has not yet been launched. I hope to launch it. The mind of so many thousand years has worked round and round inside the circle of these three ideas as a boat on an inland lake. Let us haul it over the belt of land, launch on the ocean, and sail outwards.

There is so much beyond all that has ever yet been imagined. As I write these words, in the very moment, I feel that the whole air, the sunshine out yonder lighting up the

ploughed earth, the distant sky, the circum-
ambient ether, and that far space, is full of
soul-secrets, soul-life, things outside the experience of all the ages. The fact of my
own existence as I write, as I exist at this
second, is so marvellous, so miracle-like,
strange, and supernatural to me, that I un-
hesitatingly conclude I am always on the
margin of life illimitable, and that there are
higher conditions than existence. Everything
around is supernatural; everything so full of
unexplained meaning.

Twelve thousand years since the Caveman
stood at the mouth of his cavern and gazed
out at the night and the stars. He looked
again and saw the sun rise beyond the sea.
He reposed in the noontide heat under the
shade of the trees, he closed his eyes and
looked into himself. He was face to face
with the earth, the sun, the night; face to
face with himself. There was nothing be-

tween; no wall of written tradition; no built-up system of culture—his naked mind was confronted by naked earth. He made three idea-discoveries, wresting them from the unknown; the existence of his soul, immortality, the deity. Now, to-day, as I write, I stand in exactly the same position as the Caveman. Written tradition, systems of culture, modes of thought, have for me no existence. If ever they took any hold of my mind it must have been very slight; they have long ago been erased.

From earth and sea and sun, from night, the stars, from day, the trees, the hills, from my own soul—from these I think. I stand this moment at the mouth of the ancient cave, face to face with nature, face to face with the supernatural, with myself. My naked mind confronts the unknown. I see as clearly as the noonday that this is not all; I see other and higher conditions than existence; I see not only the existence of the soul, immortality, but, in addition, I realise a soul-life illimitable; I realise the existence of a cosmos of thought; I realise the existence of an inexpressible entity infinitely higher than deity. I strive to give utterance to a Fourth Idea. The very idea that there is another idea is something gained. The three found by the Cavemen are but stepping-stones: first links of an endless chain. At the mouth of the ancient cave, face to face with the unknown, they prayed. Prone in heart to-day I pray, Give me the deepest soul-life.

CHAPTER IV

THE wind sighs through the grass, sighs
in the sunshine; it has drifted the butterfly
eastwards along the hill. A few yards away
there lies the skull of a lamb on the turf,
white and bleached, picked clean long since
by crows and ants. Like the faint ripple of
the summer sea sounding in the hollow of
the ear, so the sweet air ripples in the grass.
The ashes of the man interred in the tumulus
are indistinguishable; they have sunk away
like rain into the earth; so his body has
disappeared. I am under no delusion; I
am fully aware that no demonstration can
be given of the three stepping-stones of the
Cavemen. The soul is inscrutable; it is not
in evidence to show that it exists; immor-

tality is not tangible. Full well I know that
reason and knowledge and experience tend
to disprove all three; that experience denies
answer to prayer. I am under no delusion
whatever; I grasp death firmly in conception
as I can grasp this bleached bone; utter
extinction, annihilation. That the soul is a
product at best of organic composition; that
it goes out like a flame. This may be the
end; my soul may sink like rain into the
earth and disappear. Wind and earth, sea,
and night and day, what then? Let my
soul be but a product, what then? I say
it is nothing to me; this only I know, that
while I have lived—now, this moment, while
I live—I think immortality, I lift my mind
to a Fourth Idea. If I pass into utter
oblivion, yet I have had that.

The original three ideas of the Cavemen.
became encumbered with superstition; ritual
grew up, and ceremony, and long ranks of

souls were painted on papyri waiting to be weighed in the scales, and to be punished or rewarded. These cobwebs grotesque have sullied the original discoveries and cast them into discredit. Erase them altogether, and consider only the underlying principles. The principles do not go far enough, but I shall not discard all of them for that. Even supposing the pure principles to be illusions, and annihilation the end, even then it is better — it is something gained to have thought them. Thought is life; to have thought them is to have lived them. Accepting two of them as true in principle, then I say that these are but the threshold. For twelve thousand years no effort has been made to get beyond that threshold. These are but the primer of soul-life; the merest hieroglyphics chipped out, a little shape given to the unknown.

Not to-morrow but to-day. Not the

to-morrow of the tumulus, the hour of the sunshine now. This moment give me to live soul-life, not only after death. Now is eternity, now I am in the midst of immortality; now the supernatural crowds around me. Open my mind, give my soul to see, let me live it now on earth, while I hear the burring of the larger bees, the sweet air in the grass, and watch the yellow wheat wave beneath me. Sun and earth and sea, night and day—these are the least of things. Give me soul-life.

There is nothing human in nature. The earth, though loved so dearly, would let me perish on the ground, and neither bring forth food nor water. Burning in the sky the great sun, of whose company I have been so fond, would merely burn on and make no motion to assist me. Those who have been in an open boat at sea without water have proved the mercies of the sun, and of the deity who did not give them one drop of rain, dying in misery under the same rays that smile so beautifully on the flowers. In the south the sun is the enemy; night and coolness and rain are the friends of man. As for the sea, it offers us salt water which we cannot drink. The trees care nothing for us; the hill I visited so often in days gone by has not missed me. The sun scorches man, and will in his naked state roast him alive. The sea and the fresh water alike make no effort to uphold him if his vessel founders; he casts up his arms in vain, they come to their level over his head, filling the spot his body occupied. If he falls from a cliff the air parts; the earth beneath dashes him to pieces.

Water he can drink, but it is not produced for him; how many thousands have perished for want of it? Some fruits are produced which he can eat, but they do not produce themselves for him; merely for the purpose of continuing their species. In wild, tropical countries, at the first glance there appears to be some consideration for him, but it is on the surface only. The lion pounces on him, the rhinoceros crushes him, the serpent bites, insects torture, diseases rack him. Disease worked its dreary will even among the flower-crowned Polynesians. Returning to our own country, this very thyme which scents my fingers did not grow for that purpose, but for its own. So does the wheat beneath; we utilise it, but its original and native purpose was for itself. By night it is the same as by day; the stars care not, they pursue their courses revolving, and we are nothing to them. There is nothing human in the whole round of nature. All nature, all the universe that we can see, is absolutely indifferent to us, and except to us human life is of no more value than grass. If the entire human race perished at this hour, what difference would it make to the earth? What would the earth care? As much as for the extinct dodo, or for the fate of the elephant now going.

On the contrary, a great part, perhaps the whole, of nature and of the universe is distinctly anti-human. The term inhuman does not express my meaning, anti-human is better; outre-human, in the sense of beyond, outside, almost grotesque in its attitude towards, would nearly convey it. Everything is anti-human. How extraordinary, strange, and incomprehensible are the creatures captured out of the depths of the sea! The distorted fishes; the ghastly cuttles; the hideous eel-like shapes; the crawling shell-encrusted things; the centipede-like beings; monstrous forms, to see which gives a shock to the brain. They shock the mind because they exhibit an absence of design. There is no idea in them.

They have no shape, form, grace, or purpose; they call up a vague sense of chaos,
chaos which the mind revolts from. It would
be a relief to the thought if they ceased to
be, and utterly disappeared from the sea.
They are not inimical of intent towards man,
not even the shark; but there the shark is,
and that is enough. These miserably hideous
things of the sea are not anti-human in the
sense of persecution, they are outside, they
are ultra and beyond. It is like looking into
chaos, and it is vivid because these creatures,
interred alive a hundred fathoms deep, are
seldom seen; so that the mind sees them as
if only that moment they had come into existence. Use has not habituated it to them,
so that their anti-human character is at once
apparent, and stares at us with glassy eye.

But it is the same in reality with the
creatures on the earth. There are some of
these even now to which use has not accus-

tomed the mind. Such, for instance, as the toad. At its shapeless shape appearing in an unexpected corner many people start and exclaim. They are aware that they shall receive no injury from it, yet it affrights them, it sends a shock to the mind. The reason lies in its obviously anti-human character. All the designless, formless chaos of chance-directed matter, without idea or human plan, squats there embodied in the pathway. By watching the creature, and convincing the mind from observation that it is harmless, and even has uses, the horror wears away. But still remains the form to which the mind can never reconcile itself. Carved in wood it is still repellent.

Or suddenly there is a rustle like a faint hiss in the grass, and a green snake glides over the bank. The breath in the chest seems to lose its vitality; for an instant the nerves refuse to transmit the force of life.

The gliding yellow - streaked worm is so utterly opposed to the ever present Idea in the mind. Custom may reduce the horror, but no long pondering can ever bring that creature within the pale of the human Idea. These are so distinctly opposite and anti-human that thousands of years have not sufficed to soften their outline. Various insects and creeping creatures excite the same sense in lesser degrees. Animals and birds in general do not. The tiger is dreaded, but causes no disgust. The exception is in those that feed on offal. Horses and dogs we love; we not only do not recognise anything opposite in them, we come to love them.

They are useful to us, they show more or less sympathy with us, they possess, especially the horse, a certain grace of movement. A gloss, as it were, is thrown over them by these attributes and by familiarity. The shape of the horse to the eye has become conventional: it is accepted. Yet the horse is not in any sense human. Could we look at it suddenly, without previous acquaintance, as at strange fishes in a tank, the ultra-human character of the horse would be apparent. It is the curves of the neck and body that carry the horse past without adverse comment. Examine the hind legs in detail, and the curious backward motion, the shape and anti-human curves become apparent. Dogs take us by their intelligence, but they have no hand; pass the hand over the dog's head, and the shape of the skull to the sense of feeling is almost as repellent as the form of the toad to the sense of sight. We have gradually gathered around us all the creatures that are less markedly anti-human, horses and dogs and birds, but they are still themselves. They originally existed like the wheat, for themselves; we utilise them, but they are not of us.

There is nothing human in any living animal. All nature, the universe as far as we see, is anti- or ultra-human, outside, and has no concern with man. These things are unnatural to him. By no course of reasoning, however tortuous, can nature and the universe be fitted to the mind. Nor can the mind be fitted to the cosmos. My mind cannot be twisted to it; I am separate altogether from these designless things. The soul cannot be wrested down to them. The laws of nature are of no importance to it. I refuse to be bound by the laws of the tides, nor am I so bound. Though bodily swung round on this rotating globe, my mind always remains in the centre. No tidal law, no rotation, no gravitation can control my thought.

Centuries of thought have failed to reconcile and fit the mind to the universe, which is designless, and purposeless, and without idea. I will not endeavour to fit my thought to it any longer; I find and believe myself to be distinct—separate; and I will labour in earnest to obtain the highest culture for myself. As these natural things have no connection with man, it follows again that the natural is the strange and mysterious, and the supernatural the natural.

There being nothing human in nature or the universe, and all things being ultra-human and without design, shape, or purpose, I conclude that no deity has anything to do with nature. There is no god in nature, nor in any matter anywhere, either in the clods on the earth or in the composition of the stars. For what we understand by the deity is the purest form of Idea, of Mind, and no mind is exhibited in these. That which controls them is distinct altogether from deity. It is not force in the sense of electricity, nor a deity as god, nor a spirit, not even an intelligence, but a power quite different to anything yet imagined. I cease, therefore, to look for deity in nature or the cosmos at large, or to trace any marks of divine handi-work. I search for traces of this force which is not god, and is certainly not the higher than deity of whom I have written. It is a force without a mind. I wish to indicate something more subtle than electricity, but absolutely devoid of consciousness, and with no more feeling than the force which lifts the tides.

Next, in human affairs, in the relations of man with man, in the conduct of life, in the events that occur, in human affairs generally, everything happens by chance. No prudence in conduct, no wisdom or foresight can effect anything, for the most trivial circumstance will upset the deepest plan of the wisest mind. As Xenophon observed in old times, wisdom is like casting dice and determining your course by the number that appears. Virtue, humanity, the best and most beautiful conduct is wholly in vain. The history of thousands of years demonstrates it. In all these years there is no more moving instance on record than that of Danae, when she was dragged to the precipice, two thousand years ago. Sophron was governor of Ephesus, and Laodice plotted to assassinate him. Danae discovered the plot, and warned Sophron, who fled, and saved his life. Laodice—the murderess in intent—had Danae seized and cast from a cliff. On the verge Danae said that some persons despised the deity, and they might now prove the justice of their contempt by her fate. For having saved the man who was to her as a husband, she was rewarded in this way with cruel death by the deity, but Laodice was advanced to honour. The bitterness of these words remains to this hour.

In truth the deity, if responsible for such a thing, or for similar things which occur now, should be despised. One must always despise the fatuous belief in such a deity. But as everything in human affairs obviously happens by chance, it is clear that no deity is responsible. If the deity guides chance in that manner, then let the deity be despised. Apparently the deity does not interfere, and all things happen by chance. I cease, therefore, to look for traces of the deity in life, because no such traces exist.

I conclude that there is an existence, a something higher than soul—higher, better, and more perfect than deity. Earnestly I pray to find this something better than a god. There is something superior, higher, more good. For this I search, labour, think, and pray. If after all there be nothing, and my soul has to go out like a flame, yet even then I have thought this while it lives. With the whole force of my existence, with the whole force of my thought, mind, and soul, I pray to find this Highest Soul, this greater than deity, this better than god. Give me to live the deepest soul-life now and always with this Soul. For want of words I write soul, but I think that it is something beyond soul.

CHAPTER V

IT is not possible to narrate these incidents of the mind in strict order. I must now return to a period earlier than anything already narrated, and pass in review other phases of my search from then up till recently. So long since that I have forgotten the date, I used every morning to visit a spot where I could get a clear view of the east. Immediately on rising I went out to some elms; thence I could see across the dewy fields to the distant hill over or near which the sun rose. These elms partially hid me, for at that time I had a dislike to being seen, feeling that I should be despised if I was noticed. This happened once or twice, and I knew I was watched contemptuously, though no one had the least idea of my object. But I went every morning, and was satisfied if I could get two or three minutes to think unchecked. Often I saw the sun rise over the line of the hills, but if it was summer the sun had been up a long time.

I looked at the hills, at the dewy grass, and then up through the elm branches to the sky. In a moment all that was behind me, the house, the people, the sounds, seemed to disappear, and to leave me alone. Involuntarily I drew a long breath, then I breathed slowly. My thought, or inner consciousness, went up through the illumined sky, and I was lost in a moment of exaltation. This only lasted a very short time, perhaps only part of a second, and while it lasted there was no formulated wish. I was absorbed; I drank the beauty of the morning; I was exalted. When it ceased I did wish for some increase or enlargement of my existence to

correspond with the largeness of feeling I
had momentarily enjoyed. Sometimes the
wind came through the tops of the elms,
and the slender boughs bent, and gazing up
through them, and beyond the fleecy clouds,
I felt lifted up. The light coming across the
grass and leaving itself on the dew-drops, the
sound of the wind, and the sense of mounting
to the lofty heaven, filled me with a deep
sigh, a wish to draw something out of the
beauty of it, some part of that which caused
my admiration, the subtle inner essence.

Sometimes the green tips of the highest
boughs seemed gilded, the light laid a gold
on the green. Or the trees bowed to a
stormy wind roaring through them, the grass
threw itself down, and in the east broad cur-
tains of a rosy tint stretched along. The
light was turned to redness in the vapour, and
rain hid the summit of the hill. In the rush
and roar of the stormy wind the same exalta-

tion, the same desire, lifted me for a moment. I went there every morning, I could not exactly define why; it was like going to a rose bush to taste the scent of the flower and feel the dew from its petals on the lips. But I desired the beauty—the inner subtle meaning—to be in me, that I might have it, and with it an existence of a higher kind.

Later on I began to have daily pilgrimages to think these things. There was a feeling that I must go somewhere, and be alone. It was a necessity to have a few minutes of this separate life every day; my mind required to live its own life apart from other things. A great oak at a short distance was one resort, and sitting on the grass at the roots, or leaning against the trunk and looking over the quiet meadows towards the bright southern sky, I could live my own life a little while. Behind the trunk I was alone; I liked to lean against it; to touch the lichen on the rough bark. High in the wood of branches the birds were not alarmed; they sang, or called, and passed to and fro happily. The wind moved the leaves, and they replied to it softly; and now at this distance of time I can see the fragments of sky up through the boughs. Bees were always humming in the green field; ring-doves went over swiftly, flying for the woods.

Of the sun I was conscious; I could not look at it, but the boughs held back the beams so that I could feel the sun's presence pleasantly. They shaded the sun, yet let me know that it was there. There came to me a delicate, but at the same time a deep, strong, and sensuous enjoyment of the beautiful green earth, the beautiful sky and sun; I felt them, they gave me inexpressible delight, as if they embraced and poured out their love upon me. It was I who loved them, for my heart was broader than the earth; it is broader now than even then, more thirsty and desirous. After the sensuous enjoyment always came the thought, the desire: That I might be like this; that I might have the inner meaning of the sun, the light, the earth, the trees and grass, translated into some growth of excellence in myself, both of body and of mind; greater perfection of physique, greater perfection of mind and soul; that I might be higher in myself. To this oak I came daily for a long time; sometimes only for a minute, for just to view the spot was enough. In the bitter cold of spring, when the north wind blackened everything, I used to come now and then at night to look from under the bare branches at the splendour of the southern sky. The stars burned with brilliance, broad Orion and flashing Sirius—there are more or brighter constellations visible then than all the year: and the clearness of the air and the blackness of the sky—black, not clouded—let them gleam in their fulness. They lifted me —they gave me fresh vigour of soul. Not all that the stars could have given, had they been destinies, could have satiated me. This, all this, and more, I wanted in myself.

There was a place a mile or so along the road where the hills could be seen much better; I went there frequently to think the same thought. Another spot was by an elm, a very short walk, where openings in the trees, and the slope of the ground, brought the hills well into view. This, too, was a favourite thinking-place. Another was a wood, half an hour's walk distant, through part of which a rude track went, so that it was not altogether inclosed. The ash-saplings, and the trees, the firs, the hazel bushes—to be among these enabled me to be myself. From the buds of spring to the berries of autumn, I always liked to

D

be there. Sometimes in spring there was a sheen of blue-bells covering acres; the doves cooed; the blackbirds whistled sweetly; there was a taste of green things in the air. But it was the tall firs that pleased me most; the glance rose up the flame-shaped fir-tree, tapering to its green tip, and above was the azure sky. By aid of the tree I felt the sky more. By aid of everything beautiful I felt myself, and in that intense sense of conscious-ness prayed for greater perfection of soul and body.

Afterwards, I walked almost daily more. than two miles along the road to a spot where the hills began, where from the first rise the road could be seen winding south-wards over the hills, open and uninclosed. I paused a minute or two by a clump of firs, in whose branches the wind always sighed— there is always a movement of the air on a hill. Southwards the sky was illumined by the sun, southwards the clouds moved across the opening or pass in the amphitheatre, and southwards, though far distant, was the sea. There I could think a moment. These pilgrimages gave me a few sacred minutes daily; the moment seemed holy when the thought or desire came in its full force.

A time came when, having to live in a town, these pilgrimages had to be suspended. The wearisome work on which I was engaged would not permit of them. But I used to look now and then, from a window, in the evening at a birch-tree at some distance; its graceful boughs drooped across the glow of the sunset. The thought was not suspended; it lived in me always. A bitterer time still came when it was necessary to be separated from those I loved. There is little indeed in the more immediate suburbs of London to gratify the sense of the beautiful. Yet there was a cedar by which I used to walk up and down, and think the same thoughts as under the great oak in the solitude of the sunlit meadows. In the course of slow time happier circumstances brought us together again, and, though near London, at a spot where there was easy access to meadows and woods. Hills that purify those who walk on them there were not. Still I thought my old thoughts.

I was much in London, and, engagements completed, I wandered about in the same way as in the woods of former days. From the stone bridges I looked down on the river; the gritty dust, the straws that lie on the bridges, flew up and whirled round with every gust from the flowing tide; gritty dust that settles in the nostrils and on the lips, the very residuum of all that is repulsive in the greatest city of the world. The noise of the traffic and the constant pressure from the crowds passing, their incessant and disjointed talk, could not distract me. One moment at least I had, a moment when I thought of the push of the great sea forcing the water to flow under the feet of these crowds, the distant sea strong and splendid; when I saw the sunlight gleam on the tidal wavelets; when I felt the wind, and was conscious of the earth, the sea, the sun, the air, the immense forces working on, while the city hummed by the river. Nature was deepened by the crowds and foot-worn stones. If the tide had ebbed, and the masts of the vessels were tilted as the hulls rested on the shelving mud, still even the blackened mud did not prevent me seeing the water as water flowing to the sea. The sea had drawn down, and the wavelets washing the strand here as they hastened were running the faster to it. Eastwards from London Bridge the river raced to the ocean.

The bright morning sun of summer heated the eastern parapet of London Bridge; I stayed in the recess to acknowledge it. The smooth water was a broad sheen of light, the built-up river flowed calm and silent by a thousand doors, rippling only where the stream chafed against a chain. Red pennants drooped, gilded vanes gleamed on polished masts, black-pitched hulls glistened like a black rook's feathers in sunlight; the clear air cut out the forward angles of the warehouses, the shadowed wharves were quiet in shadows that carried light; far down the ships that were hauling out moved in repose, and with the stream floated away into the summer mist. There was a faint blue colour in the air hovering between the built-up banks, against the lit walls, in the hollows of the houses. The swallows wheeled and climbed, twittered and glided downwards. Burning on, the great sun stood

in the sky, heating the parapet, glowing stead-
fastly upon me as when I rested in the
narrow valley grooved out in prehistoric times.
Burning on steadfast, and ever present as my
thought. Lighting the broad river, the broad
walls ; lighting the least speck of dust;
lighting the great heaven; gleaming on my
finger-nail. The fixed point of day—the
sun. I was intensely conscious of it; I felt
it; I felt the presence of the immense
powers of the universe; I felt out into the
depths of the ether. So intensely conscious
of the sun, the sky, the limitless space, I felt
too in the midst of eternity then, in the
midst of the supernatural, among the immortal, and the greatness of the material
realised the spirit. By these I saw my soul;
by these I knew the supernatural to be more
intensely real than the sun. I touched the
supernatural, the immortal, there that moment.

When, weary of walking on the pavements, I went to rest in the National Gallery, I sat and rested before one or other of the human pictures. I am not a picture lover: they are flat surfaces, but those that I call human are nevertheless beautiful. The knee in Daphnis and Chloe and the breast are like living things ; they draw the heart towards them, the heart must love them. I lived in looking; without beauty there is no life for me, the divine beauty of flesh is life itself to me. The shoulder in the Surprise, the rounded rise of the bust, the exquisite tints of the ripe skin, momentarily gratified the sea-thirst in me. For I thirst with all the thirst of the salt sea, and the sun-heated sands dry for the tide, with all the sea I thirst for beauty. And I know full well that one lifetime, however long, cannot fill my heart. My throat and tongue and whole body have often been parched and feverish dry with this measureless thirst, and again moist to the fingers' ends like a sappy bough. It burns in me as the sun burns in the sky.

The glowing face of Cytherea in Titian's Venus and Adonis, the heated cheek, the lips that kiss each eye that gazes on them, the desiring glance, the golden hair—sunbeams moulded into features—this face answered me. Juno's wide back and mesial groove, is any thing so lovely as the back? Cytherea's poised hips unveiled for judgment; these called up the same thirst I felt on the green sward in the sun, on the wild beach listening to the quiet sob as the summer wave drank at the land. I will search the world through for beauty. I came here and sat to rest before these in the days when I could not afford to buy so much as a glass of ale, weary and faint from walking on stone pavements. I came later on, in better times, often straight from labours which though necessary will ever be distasteful, always to rest my heart with loveliness. I go still; the divine beauty of flesh is life itself to me. It was, and is, one of my London pilgrimages.

Another was to the Greek sculpture galleries in the British Museum. The statues are not, it is said, the best; broken too, and mutilated, and seen in a dull, commonplace light. But they were shape— divine shape of man and woman; the form of limb and torso, of bust and neck, gave me a sighing sense of rest. These were they who would have stayed with me under the shadow of the oaks while the blackbirds fluted and the south air swung the cowslips. They would have walked with me among the reddened gold of the wheat. They would have rested with me on the hill-tops and in the narrow valley grooved of ancient times. They would have listened with me to the sob of the summer sea drinking the land. These had thirsted of sun, and earth, and sea, and sky. Their shape spoke this thirst and desire like mine—if I had lived with them from Greece till now I should not have had enough of them. Tracing the form of limb and torso with the eye gave me a sense of rest.

Sometimes I came in from the crowded streets and ceaseless hum; one glance at these shapes and I became myself. Sometimes I came from the Reading-room, where under the dome I often looked up from the desk and realised the crushing hopelessness of books, useless, not equal to one bubble borne along on the running brook I had walked by, giving no thought like the spring when I lifted the water in my hand and saw the light gleam on it. Torso and limb, bust and neck instantly returned me to myself; I felt as I did lying on the turf listening to the wind among the grass; it would have seemed natural to have found butterflies fluttering among the statues. The same deep desire was with me. I shall always go to speak to them; they are a place of pilgrimage; wherever there is a beautiful statue there is a place of pilgrimage.

I always stepped aside, too, to look awhile at the head of Julius Cæsar. The domes of the swelling temples of his broad head are full of mind, evident to the eye as a globe is full of substance to the sense of feeling in the hands that hold it. The thin worn cheek is entirely human; endless difficulties surmounted by endless labour are marked in it, as the sandblast, by dint of particles ceaselessly driven, carves the hardest material. If circumstances favoured him he made those circumstances his own by marvellous labour, so as justly to receive the credit of chance. Therefore the thin cheek is entirely human—the sum of human life made visible in one face—labour, and endurance, and mind, and all in vain. A shadow of deep sadness has gathered on it in the years that have passed, because endurance was without avail. It is sadder to look at than the grass-grown tumulus I used to sit by, because it is a personality, and also on account of the extreme folly of our human race ever destroying our greatest.

Far better had they endeavoured, however hopelessly, to keep him living till this day. Did but the race this hour possess one-hundredth part of his breadth of view, how happy for them! Of whom else can it be said that he had no enemies to forgive because he recognised no enemy? Nineteen hundred years ago he put in actual practice, with more arbitrary power than any despot, those very principles of humanity which are now put forward as the highest culture. But he made them to be actual things under his sway.

The one man filled with mind; the one man without avarice, anger, pettiness, littleness; the one man generous and truly great of all history. It is enough to make one despair to think of the mere brutes butting to death the great-minded Cæsar. He comes nearest to the ideal of a design-power arranging the affairs of the world for good in practical things. Before his face—the divine brow of mind above, the human suffering-drawn cheek beneath—my own thought became set and strengthened. That I could but look at things in the broad way he did; that I could not possess one particle of such width of intellect to guide my own course, to cope with and drag forth from the iron-resisting forces of the universe some one thing of my prayer for the soul and for the flesh.

CHAPTER VI

THERE is a place in front of the Royal Exchange where the wide pavement reaches out like a promontory. It is in the shape of a triangle with a rounded apex. A stream of traffic runs on either side, and other streets send their currents down into the open space before it. Like the spokes of a wheel converging streams of human life flow into this agitated pool. Horses and carriages, carts, vans, omnibuses, cabs, every kind of conveyance cross each other's course in every possible direction. Twisting in and out by the wheels and under the horses' heads, working a devious way, men and women of all conditions wind a path over. They fill the interstices between the carriages and blacken the surface, till the vans almost float on human beings. Now the streams slacken, and now they rush amain, but never cease; dark waves are always rolling down the incline opposite, waves swell out from the side rivers, all London converges into this focus. There is an indistinguishable noise—it is not clatter, hum, or roar, it is not resolvable; made up of a thousand thousand footsteps, from a thousand hoofs, a thousand wheels— of haste, and shuffle, and quick movements, and ponderous loads; no attention can resolve it into a fixed sound.

Blue carts and yellow omnibuses, varnished carriages and brown vans, green omnibuses and red cabs, pale loads of yellow straw, rusty-red iron clanking on paintless carts, high white wool-packs, grey horses, bay horses, black teams; sunlight sparkling on brass harness, gleaming from carriage panels; jingle, jingle, jingle! An intermixed and intertangled, ceaselessly changing jingle, too, of colour ; flecks of . colour champed, as it were, like bits in the horses' teeth, frothed and strewn about, and a surface always of dark-dressed people winding like the curves on fast-flowing water. This is the vortex and whirlpool, the centre of human life to-day on the earth. 'Now the tide rises and now it sinks, but the flow of these rivers always continues. Here it seethes and whirls, not for an hour only, but for all present time, hour by hour, day by day, year by year.

Here it rushes and pushes, the atoms triturate and grind, and, eagerly thrusting by, pursue their separate ends. Here it appears in its unconcealed personality, indifferent to all else but itself, absorbed and rapt in eager self, devoid and stripped of · conventional gloss and politeness, yielding only to get its own way ; driving, pushing, carried on in a stress of feverish force like a bullet, dynamic force apart from reason or will, like the force that lifts the tides and sends the clouds onwards. The friction of a thousand interests evolves a condition of electricity in which men are moved to and fro without considering their steps. Yet the agitated pool of life is stonily indifferent, the thought is absent or preoccupied, for it is evident that the mass are unconscious of the scene in which they act.

But it is more sternly real than the very stones, for all these men and women that pass through are driven on by the push of accumulated circumstances ; they cannot stay, they must go, their necks are in the slave's ring, they are beaten like seaweed against the solid walls of fact. In ancient times, Xerxes, the king of kings, looking down upon his myriads, wept to think that in a hundred years not one of them would be left. Where will be these millions of to-day in a hundred years? But, further than that, let us ask, Where then will be the sum and outcome of their labour? If they wither away like summer grass, will not at least a result be left which those of a hundred years hence may be the better for? No, not one jot! There will not be any sum or outcome or result of this ceaseless labour and movement; it vanishes in the moment that it is done, and in a hundred years nothing will be there, for nothing is there now. There will be no more sum or result than accumulates from the motion of a revolving cowl on a housetop. Nor do they receive any more sunshine during their lives, for they are unconscious of the sun.

I used to come and stand near the apex of the promontory of pavement which juts out towards the pool of life; I still go there to ponder. Burning in the sky, the sun shone on me as when I rested in the narrow valley carved in prehistoric time. Burning in the sky, I can never forget the sun. The heat of summer is dry there as if the light carried an impalpable dust; dry, breathless heat that will not let the skin respire, but swathes up the dry fire in the blood. But beyond the heat and light, I felt the presence of the sun as I felt it in the solitary valley, the presence of the resistless forces of the universe; the sun burned in the sky as I stood and pondered. Is there any theory, philosophy, or creed, is there any system . or culture, any formulated method able to meet and satisfy each separate item of this agitated pool of human life? By which they may be guided, by which hope, by which look forward? Not a mere illusion of the craven heart—something real, as real as the solid walls of fact against which, like drifted seaweed, they are dashed; something to give each separate personality sunshine and a flower in its own existence now; something to shape this million-handed labour to an end and outcome that will leave more sunshine and more flowers to those who must succeed? Something real now, and not in the spirit-land; in this hour now, as I stand and the sun burns. Can any creed, philosophy, system, or culture endure the test and remain unmolten in this fierce focus of human life?

Consider, is there anything slowly painted on the once mystic and now commonplace papyri of ancient, ancient Egypt, held on the mummy's withered breast? In that elaborate ritual, in the procession of the symbols, in the winged circle, in the laborious sarcophagus? Nothing; absolutely nothing! Before the fierce heat of the human furnace, the papyri smoulder away as paper smoulders under a lens in the sun. Remember Nineveh and the cult of the fir-cone, the turbaned and bearded bulls of stone, the lion hunt, the painted chambers loaded with tile books, the lore of the arrow-headed writing. What is in Assyria? There are sand, and failing rivers, and in Assyria's writings an utter nothing. The aged caves of India, who shall tell when they were sculptured? Far back when the sun was burning, burning in the sky as now in untold precedent time. Is there any meaning in those ancient caves? The indistinguishable noise not to be resolved, born of the human struggle, mocks in answer.

In the strange characters of the Zend, in the Sanscrit, in the effortless creed of Confucius, in the Aztec coloured-string writings and rayed stones, in the uncertain marks left of the sunken Polynesian continent, hieroglyphs as useless as those of Memphis, nothing. Nothing! They have been tried, and were found an illusion. Think then, to-day, now looking from this apex of the pavement promontory outwards from our own land to the utmost bounds of the farthest sail, is there any faith or culture at this hour which can stand in this fierce heat? From the various forms of Semitic, Aryan, or Turanian creed now existing, from the printing-press to the palm-leaf volume on to those who call on the jewel in the lotus, can aught be gathered which can face this, the Reality? The indistinguishable noise, non-resolvable, roars a loud contempt.

Turn, then, to the calm reasoning of Aristotle; is there anything in that? Can the half-divine thought of Plato, rising in storeys of sequential ideas, following each other to the conclusion, endure here? No! All the philosophers in Diogenes Laertius fade away: the theories of mediæval days; the organon of experiment; down to this hour—they are useless alike. The science of this hour, drawn from the printing-press in an endless web of paper, is powerless here; the indistinguishable noise echoed from the smoke-shadowed walls despises the whole. A thousand footsteps, a thousand hoofs, a thousand wheels roll over and utterly contemn them in complete annihilation. Mere illusions of heart or mind, they are tested and thrust aside by the irresistible push of a million converging feet.

Burning in the sky, the sun shines as it shone on me in the solitary valley, as it burned on when the earliest cave of India was carved. Above the indistinguishable roar of the many feet I feel the presence of the sun, of the immense forces of the universe, and beyond these the sense of the eternal now, of the immortal. Full well aware that all has failed, yet, side by side with the sadness of that knowledge, there lives on in me an unquenchable belief, thought burning like the sun, that there is yet something to be found, something real, something to give each separate personality sunshine and flowers in its own existence now. Something to shape this million-handed labour to an end and outcome, leaving accumulated sunshine and flowers to those who shall succeed. It must be dragged forth by might of thought from the immense forces of the universe.

To prepare for such an effort, first the mind must be cleared of the conceit that, because we live to-day, we are wiser than the ages gone. The mind must acknowledge its ignorance; all the learning and lore of so many eras must be erased from it as an encumbrance. It is not from past or present knowledge, science or faith, that it is to be drawn. Erase these altogether as they are erased under the fierce heat of the focus before me. Begin wholly afresh. Go straight to the sun, the immense forces of the universe, to the Entity unknown; go higher than a god; deeper than prayer; and open a new day. That I might but have a fragment of Cæsar's intellect to find a fragment of this desire!

From my home near London I made a pilgrimage almost daily to an aspen by a brook. It was a mile and a quarter along the road, far enough for me to walk off the concentration of mind necessary for work. The idea of the pilgrimage was to get away from the endless and nameless circumstances of everyday existence, which by degrees build a wall about the mind so that it travels in a constantly narrowing circle. This tether of the faculties tends to make them accept present knowledge, and present things, as all that can be attained to. This is all—there is nothing more—is the iterated preaching of house-life. Remain; be content; go round and round in one barren path, a little money, a little food and sleep, some ancient fables, old age and death. Of all the inventions of casuistry with which man for ages has in various ways manacled himself, and stayed his own advance, there is none equally potent with the supposition that nothing more is possible. Once well impress on the mind that it has already all, that advance is impossible because there is nothing further, and it is chained like a horse to an iron pin in the ground. It is the most deadly—the most fatal poison of the mind. No such casuistry has ever for a moment held me, but still, if permitted, the constant routine of house-life, the same work, the same thought in the work, the little circumstances regularly recurring, will dull the keenest edge of thought. By my daily pilgrimage, I escaped from it back to the sun.

In summer the leaves of the aspen rustled pleasantly, there was the tinkle of falling water over a hatch, thrushes sang and blackbirds whistled, greenfinches laughed in their talk to each other. The commonplace dusty road was commonplace no longer. In the dust was the mark of the chaffinches' little feet; the white light rendered even the dust brighter to look on. The air came from the south-west—there were distant hills in that direction—over fields of grass and corn. As I visited the spot from day to day the wheat grew from green to yellow, the wild roses flowered, the scarlet poppies appeared, and again the beeches reddened in autumn. In the march of time there fell away from my mind, as the leaves from the trees in autumn, the last traces and relics of superstitions and traditions acquired compulsorily in childhood. Always feebly adhering, they finally disappeared.

There fell away, too, personal bias and prejudices, enabling me to see clearer and with wider sympathies. The glamour of modern science and discoveries faded away, for I found them no more than the first potter's wheel. Erasure and reception proceeded together; the past accumulations of casuistry were erased, and my thought widened to receive the idea of something beyond all previous ideas. With disbelief, belief increased. The aspiration and hope, the prayer, was the same as that which I felt years before on the hills, only it now broadened.

Experience of life, instead of curtailing and checking my prayer, led me to reject experience altogether. As well might the horse believe that the road the bridle forces it to traverse every day encircles the earth as I believe in experience. All the experience of the greatest city in the world could not withhold me. I rejected it wholly. I stood bare-headed before the sun, in the presence of the earth and air, in the presence of the immense forces of the universe. I demand that which will make me more perfect now, this hour. London convinced me of my own thought. That thought has always been with me, and always grows wider.

One midsummer I went out of the road into the fields, and sat down on the grass between the yellowing wheat and the green hawthorn bushes. The sun burned in the sky, the wheat was full of a luxuriant sense of growth, the grass high, the earth giving its vigour to tree and leaf, the heaven blue. The vigour and growth, the warmth and light, the beauty and richness of it entered into me; an ecstasy of soul accompanied the delicate excitement of the senses: the soul rose with the body. Rapt in the fulness of the moment, I prayed there with all that expansion of mind and frame; no words, no definition, in-expressible desire of physical life, of soul-life, equal to and beyond the highest imagining of my heart.

These memories cannot be placed in exact chronological order. There was a time when a weary restlessness came upon me, perhaps from too-long-continued labour. It was like a drought—a moral drought—as if I had been absent for many years from the sources of life and hope. The inner nature was faint, all was dry and tasteless; I was weary for the pure, fresh springs of thought. Some instinctive feeling uncontrollable drove me to the sea; I was so under its influence that I could not arrange the journey so as to get the longest day. I merely started, and of course had to wait and endure much inconvenience. To get to the sea at some quiet spot was my one thought; to do so I had to travel farther, and from want of prearrangement it was between two and three in the afternoon before I reached the end of my journey. Even then, being too much preoccupied to inquire the way, I missed the road and had to walk a long distance before coming to the shore. But I found the sea at last; I walked beside it in a trance away from the houses out into the wheat. The ripe corn stood up to the beach, the waves on one side of the shingle, and the yellow wheat on the other.

There, alone, I went down to the sea. I stood where the foam came to my feet, and looked out over the sunlit waters. The great earth bearing the richness of the harvest, and its hills golden with corn, was at my back; its strength and firmness under me. The great sun shone above, the wide sea was before me, the wind came sweet and strong from the waves. The life of the earth and the sea, the glow of the sun filled me; I touched the surge with my hand, I lifted my face to the sun, I opened my lips to the wind. I prayed aloud in the roar of the waves—my soul was strong as the sea and prayed with the sea's might. Give me fulness of life like to the sea and the sun, to the earth and the air; give me fulness of physical life, mind equal and beyond their fulness; give me a greatness and perfection of soul higher than all things; give me my inexpressible desire which swells in me like a tide—give it to me with all the force of the sea.

Then I rested, sitting by the wheat; the bank of beach was between me and the sea, but the waves beat against it; the sea was there, the sea was present and at hand. By the dry wheat I rested, I did not think, I was inhaling the richness of the sea, all the strength and depth of meaning of the sea and earth came to me again. I rubbed out some of the wheat in my hands, I took up a piece of clod and crumbled it in my fingers—it was a joy to touch it—I held my hand so that I could see the sunlight gleam on the slightly moist surface of the skin. The earth and sun

E

were to me like my flesh and blood, and the air of the sea life.

With all the greater existence I drew from them I prayed for a bodily life equal to it, for a soul-life beyond my thought, for my inexpressible desire of more than I could shape even into idea. There was something higher than idea, invisible to thought as air to the eye; give me bodily life equal in fulness to the strength of earth, and sun, and sea; give me the soul-life of my desire. Once more I went down to the sea, touched it, and said farewell. So deep was the inhalation of this life that day, that it seemed to remain in me for years. This was a real pilgrimage.

Time passed away, with more labour, pleasure, and again at last, after much pain and weariness of mind, I came down again to the sea. The circumstances were changed —it was not a hurried glance—there were opportunities for longer thought. It mattered scarcely anything to me now whether I was alone, or whether houses and other people were near. Nothing could disturb my inner vision. By the sea, aware of the sun overhead, and the blue heaven, I feel that there is nothing between me and space. This is the verge of a gulf, and a tangent from my feet goes straight unchecked into the unknown. It is the edge of the abyss as much as if the earth were cut away in a sheer fall of eight thousand miles to the sky beneath, thence a hollow to the stars. Looking straight out is looking straight down; the eye-glance gradually departs from the sea-level, and, rising as that falls, enters the hollow of heaven. It is gazing along the face of a vast precipice into the hollow space which is nameless.

There mystery has been placed, but realising the vast hollow yonder makes me feel that the mystery is here. I, who am here on the verge, standing on the margin of the sky, am in the mystery itself. If I let my eye look back upon me from the extreme opposite of heaven, then this spot where I stand is in the centre of the hollow. Alone with the sea and sky, I presently feel all the depth and wonder of the unknown come back surging up around, and touching me as the foam runs to my feet. I am in it now, not to-morrow, this moment; I cannot escape from it. Though I may deceive myself with labour, yet still I am in it; in sleep too. There is no escape from this immensity.

Feeling this by the sea, under the sun, my life enlarges and quickens, striving to take to itself the largeness of the heaven. The frame cannot expand, but the soul is able to stand before it. No giant's body could be in proportion to the earth, but a little spirit is equal to the entire cosmos, to earth and ocean, sun and star-hollow. These are but a few acres to it. Were the cosmos twice as wide, the soul could run over it, and return to itself in a time so small, no measure exists to mete it. Therefore, I think the soul may sometimes find out an existence as superior as my mind is to the dead chalk cliff.

With the great sun burning over the foam-flaked sea, roofed with heaven — aware of myself, a consciousness forced on me by these things—I feel that thought must yet grow larger and correspond in magnitude of conception to these. But these cannot content me, these Titanic things of sea, and sun, and profundity; I feel that my thought is stronger than they are. I burn life like a torch. The hot light shot back from the sea scorches my cheek—my life is burning in me. The soul throbs like the sea for a larger life. No thought which I have ever had has satisfied my soul.

CHAPTER VII

My strength is not enough to fulfil my desire; if I had the strength of the ocean, and of the earth, the burning vigour of the sun implanted in my limbs, it would hardly suffice to gratify the measureless desire of life which possesses me. I have often walked the day long over the sward, and, compelled to pause, at length, in my weariness, I was full of the same eagerness with which I started. The sinews would obey no longer, but the will was the same. My frame could never take the violent exertion my heart demanded. Labour of body was like meat and drink to me. Over the open hills, up the steep ascents, mile after mile, there was deep enjoyment in the long-drawn breath, the spring of the foot, in the act of rapid movement. Never have I had enough of it; I wearied long before I was satisfied, and weariness did not bring a cessation of desire; the thirst was still there.

I rowed, I used the axe, I split tree-trunks with wedges; my arms tired, but my spirit remained fresh and chafed against the physical weariness. My arms were not strong enough to satisfy me with the axe, or wedges, or oars. There was delight in the moment, but it was not enough. I swam, and what is more delicious than swimming? It is exercise and luxury at once. But I could not swim far enough; I was always dissatisfied with myself on leaving the water. Nature has not given me a great frame, and had it done so I should still have longed for more. I was out of doors all day, and often half the night; still I wanted more sunshine, more air, the hours were too short. I feel

this even more now than in the violence of
early youth: the hours are too short, the
day should be sixty hours long. Slumber,
too, is abbreviated and restricted; forty hours
of night and sleep would not be too much.
So little can be accomplished in the longest
summer day, so little rest and new force
is accumulated in a short eight hours of
sleep.

I live by the sea now; I can see nothing
of it in a day; why, I do but get a breath
of it, and the sun sinks before I have well
begun to think. Life is so little and so
mean. I dream sometimes backwards of the
ancient times. If I could have the bow of
Ninus, and the earth full of wild bulls and
lions, to hunt them down, there would be rest
in that. To shoot with a gun is nothing; a
mere touch discharges it. Give me a bow,
that I may enjoy the delight of feeling myself draw the string and the strong wood

bending, that I may see the rush of the arrow, and the broad head bury itself deep in shaggy hide. Give me an iron mace that I may crush the savage beast and hammer him down. A spear to thrust through with, so that I may feel the long blade enter and the push of the shaft. The unwearied strength of Ninus to hunt unceasingly in the fierce sun. Still I should desire greater strength and a stouter bow, wilder creatures to combat. The intense life of the senses, there is never enough for them. I envy Semiramis; I would have been ten times Semiramis. I envy Nero, because of the great concourse of beauty he saw. I should like to be loved by every beautiful woman on earth, from the swart Nubian to the white and divine Greek.

Wine is pleasant and meat refreshing; but though I own with absolute honesty that I like them, these are the least of all. Of these two only have I ever had enough. The vehemence of exertion, the vehemence of the spear, the vehemence of sunlight and life, the insatiate desire of insatiate Semi-ramis, the still more insatiate desire of love, divine and beautiful, the uncontrollable adora-tion of beauty, these—these : give me these in greater abundance than was ever known to man or woman. The strength of Hercules, the fulness of the senses, the richness of life, would not in the least impair my desire of soul-life. On the reverse, with every stronger beat of the pulse my desire of soul-life would expand. So it has ever been with me; in hard exercise, in sensuous plea-sure, in the embrace of the sunlight, even in the drinking of a glass of wine, my heart has been lifted the higher towards perfection of soul. Fulness of physical life causes a deeper desire of soul-life.

Let me be physically perfect, in shape,

vigour, and movement. My frame, naturally slender, will not respond to labour, and increase in proportion to effort, nor will exposure harden a delicate skin. It disappoints me so far, but my spirit rises with the effort, and my thought opens. This is the only profit of frost, the pleasure of winter, to conquer cold, and to feel braced and strengthened by that whose province it is to wither and destroy, making of cold, life's enemy, life's renewer. The black north wind hardens the resolution as steel is tempered in ice-water. It is a sensual joy, as sensuous as the warm embrace of the sunlight, but fulness of physical life ever brings to me a more eager desire of soul-life.

Splendid it is to feel the boat rise to the roller, or forced through by the sail to shear the foam aside like a share; splendid to undulate as the chest lies on the wave, swimming, the brimming ocean round: then

I know and feel its deep strong tide, its immense fulness, and the sun glowing over; splendid to climb the steep green hill: in these I feel myself, I drink the exquisite joy of the senses, and my soul lifts itself with them. It is beautiful even to watch a fine horse gallop, the long stride, the rush of the wind as he passes—my heart beats quicker to the thud of the hoofs, and I feel his strength. Gladly would I have the strength of the Tartar stallion roaming the wild steppe; that very strength, what vehemence of soul-thought would accompany it. But I should like it, too, for itself. For I believe, with all my heart, in the body and the flesh, and believe that it should be increased and made more beautiful by every means. I believe—I do more than think— I believe it to be a sacred duty, incumbent upon every one, man and woman, to add to and encourage their physical life, by exercise, and in every manner. A sacred duty each towards himself, and each towards the whole of the human race. Each one of us should do some little part for the physical good of the race—health, strength, vigour. There is no harm therein to the soul: on the contrary, those who stunt their physical life are most certainly stunting their souls.

I believe all manner of asceticism to be the vilest blasphemy—blasphemy towards the whole of the human race. I believe in the flesh and the body, which is worthy of worship—to see a perfect human body unveiled causes a sense of worship. The ascetics are the only persons who are impure. Increase of physical beauty is attended by increase of soul beauty. The soul is the higher even by gazing on beauty. Let me be fleshly perfect.

It is in myself that I desire increase, profit, and exaltation of body, mind, and soul. The surroundings, the clothes, the dwelling, the social status, the circumstances are to me utterly indifferent. Let the floor of the room be bare, let the furniture be a plank table, the bed a mere pallet. Let the house be plain and simple, but in the midst of air and light. These are enough—a cave would be enough; in a warmer climate the open air would suffice. Let me be furnished in myself with health, safety, strength, the perfection of physical existence; let my mind be furnished with highest thoughts of soul-life. Let me be in myself myself fully. The pageantry of power, the still more foolish pageantry of wealth, the senseless precedence of place; words fail me to express my utter contempt for such pleasure or such ambitions. Let me be in myself myself fully, and those I love equally so.

It is enough to lie on the sward in the shadow of green boughs, to listen to the songs of summer, to drink in the sunlight, the air, the flowers, the sky, the beauty of all. Or upon the hill-tops to watch the white clouds rising over the curved hill-lines, their shadows descending the slope. Or on the beach to listen to the sweet sigh as the smooth sea runs up and recedes. It is lying beside the immortals, in-drawing the life of the ocean, the earth, and the sun.

I want to be always in company with these, with earth, and sun, and sea, and stars by night. The pettiness of house-life—chairs and tables—and the pettiness of observances, the petty necessity of useless labour, useless because productive of nothing, chafe me the year through. I want to be always in company with the sun, and sea, and earth. These, and the stars by night, are my natural companions.

My heart looks back and sympathises with all the joy and life of ancient time.

With the circling dance burned in still attitude on the vase; with the chase and the hunter eagerly pursuing, whose javelin trembles to be thrown; with the extreme fury of feeling, the whirl of joy in the warriors from Marathon to the last battle of Rome, not with the slaughter, but with the passion—the life in the passion; with the garlands and the flowers; with all the breathing busts that have panted beneath the sun. O beautiful human life! Tears come in my eyes as I think of it. So beautiful, so inexpressibly beautiful!

So deep is the passion of life that, if it were possible to live again, it must be exquisite to die pushing the eager breast against the sword. In the flush of strength to face the sharp pain joyously, and laugh in the last glance of the sun—if only to live again, now on earth, were possible. So subtle is the chord of life that sometimes to watch troops marching in rhythmic order, undulating along the column as the feet are lifted, brings tears in my eyes. Yet could I have in my own heart all the passion, the love and joy, burned in the breasts that have panted, breathing deeply, since the hour of Ilion, yet still I should desire more. How willingly I would strew the paths of all with flowers; how beautiful a delight to make the world joyous! The song should never be silent, the dance never still, the laugh should sound like water which runs for ever.

I would submit to a severe discipline, and to go without many things cheerfully, for the good and happiness of the human race in the future. Each one of us should do something, however small, towards that great end. At the present time the labour of our predecessors in this country, in all other countries of the earth, is entirely wasted. We live— that is, we snatch an existence—and our works become nothing. The piling up of fortunes, the building of cities, the establishment of immense commerce, ends in a cipher. These objects are so outside my idea that I cannot understand them, and look upon the struggle in amazement. Not even the pressure of poverty can force upon me an understanding of, and sympathy with, these things. It is the human being as the human being of whom I think. That the human being as the human being, nude—apart altogether from money, clothing, houses, properties— should enjoy greater health, strength, safety, beauty, and happiness, I would gladly agree to a discipline like that of Sparta. The Spartan method did produce the finest race of men, and Sparta was famous in antiquity for the most beautiful women. So far, therefore, it fits exactly to my ideas.

No science of modern times has yet discovered a plan to meet the requirements of the millions who live now, no plan by which they might attain similar physical proportion. Some increase of longevity, some slight improvement in the general health is promised, and these are great things, but far, far beneath the ideal. Probably the whole mode of thought of the nations must be altered before physical progress is possible. Not while money, furniture, affected show and the pageantry of wealth are the ambitions of the multitude can the multitude become ideal in form. When the ambition of the multitude is fixed on the ideal of form and beauty, then that ideal will become immediately possible, and a marked advance towards it could be made in three generations. Glad, indeed, should I be to discover something that would help towards this end.

How pleasant it would be each day to think, To-day I have done something that will tend to render future generations more happy. The very thought would make this hour sweeter. It is absolutely necessary that something of this kind should be discovered. First, we must lay down the axiom that as yet nothing has been found; we have nothing to start with; all has to be begun afresh. All courses or methods of human life have hitherto been failures. Some course of life is needed based on things that are, irrespective of tradition. The physical ideal must be kept steadily in view.

CHAPTER VIII

AN enumeration of the useless would almost be an enumeration of everything hitherto pursued. For instance, to go back as far as possible, the study and labour expended on Egyptian inscriptions and papyri, which contain nothing but doubtful, because laudatory history, invocations to idols, and similar matters: all these labours are in vain. Take a broom and sweep the papyri away into the dust. The Assyrian terra-cotta tablets, some recording fables, and some even sadder —contracts between men whose bodies were dust twenty centuries since—take a hammer and demolish them. Set a battery to beat down the pyramids, and a mind-battery to destroy the deadening influence of tradition.

The Greek statue lives to this day, and has the highest use of all, the use of true beauty. The Greek and Roman philosophers have the value of furnishing the mind with material to think from. Egyptian and Assyrian, mediæval and eighteenth-century culture, miscalled, are all alike mere dust, and absolutely useless.

There is a mass of knowledge so called at the present day equally useless, and nothing but an encumbrance. We are forced by circumstances to become familiar with it, but the time expended on it is lost. No physical ideal—far less any soul-ideal—will ever be reached by it. In a recent generation erudition in the text of the classics was considered the most honourable of pursuits; certainly nothing could be less valuable. In our own generation, another species of erudition is lauded—erudition in the laws of matter—which, in itself, is but one degree better. The study of matter for matter's sake is despicable; if any can turn that study to advance the ideal of life, it immediately becomes most valuable. But not without the human ideal. It is nothing to me if the planets revolve around the sun, or the sun around the earth, unless I can thereby gather an increase of body or mind. As the conception of the planets revolving around the sun, the present astronomical conception of the heavens, is distinctly grander than that of Ptolemy, it is therefore superior, and a gain to the human mind. So with other sciences, not immediately useful, yet if they furnish the mind with material of thought, they are an advance.

But not in themselves—only in conjunction with the human ideal. Once let that slip out of the thought, and science is of no more use than the invocations in the Egyptian papyri. The world would be the gainer if

the Nile rose and swept away pyramid and
tomb, sarcophagus, papyri, and inscription;
for it seems as if most of the superstitions
which still to this hour, in our own country,
hold minds in their sway, originated in
Egypt. The world would be the gainer if a
Nile flood of new thought arose and swept
away the past, concentrating the effort of all
the races of the earth upon man's body, that
it might reach an ideal of shape, and health,
and happiness.

Nothing is of any use unless it gives me
a stronger body and mind, a more beautiful
body, a happy existence, and a soul-life now.
The last phase of philosophy is equally useless with the rest. The belief that the human
mind was evolved, in the process of un-
numbered years, from a fragment of pal-
pitating slime through a thousand gradations,
is a modern superstition, and proceeds upon
assumption alone.

Nothing is evolved, no evolution takes place, there is no record of such an event; it is pure assertion. The theory fascinates many, because they find, upon study of physiology, that the gradations between animal and vegetable are so fine and so close together, as if a common web bound them together. But although they stand so near they never change places. They are like the figures on the face of a clock; there are minute dots between, apparently connecting each with the other, and the hands move round over all. Yet ten never becomes twelve, and each second even is parted from the next, as you may hear by listening to the beat. So the gradations of life, past and present, though standing close together never change places. Nothing is evolved. There is no evolution any more than there is any design in nature. By standing face to face with nature, and not from books, I have convinced myself that there is no design and no evolution. What there is, what was the cause, how and why, is not yet known; certainly it was neither of these.

But it may be argued the world must have been created, or it must have been made of existing things, or it must have been evolved, or it must have existed for ever, through all eternity. I think not. I do not think that either of these are " musts," nor that any " must " has yet been discovered; not even that there " must " be a first cause. There may be other things—other physical forces even—of which we know nothing. I strongly suspect there are. There may be other ideas altogether from any we have hitherto had the use of. For many ages our ideas have been confined to two or three. We have conceived the idea of creation, which is the highest and grandest of all, if not historically true; we have conceived the idea of design, that is of an intelligence making order and revolution of chaos; and we have conceived the idea of evolution by physical laws of matter, which, though now so much insisted on, is as ancient as the Greek philosophers. But there may be another alternative; I think there are other alternatives.

Whenever the mind obtains a wider view we may find that origin, for instance, is not always due to what is understood by cause. At this moment the mind is unable to conceive of anything happening, or of anything coming into existence, without a cause. From cause to effect is the sequence of our ideas. But I think that if at some time we should obtain an altogether different and broader sequence of ideas, we may discover that there are various other alternatives. As the world, and the universe at large, was not constructed according to plan, so it is clear that the sequence or circle of ideas which includes plan, and cause, and effect, are not in the circle of ideas which would correctly explain it. Put aside the plan-circle of ideas, and it will at once be evident that there is no inherent necessity or "must." There is no inherent necessity for a first cause, or that the world and the universe was created, or that it was shaped of existing matter, or that it evolved itself and its inhabitants, or that the cosmos has existed in varying forms for ever. There may be other alternatives altogether. The only idea I can give is the idea that there is another idea.

In this "must"—"it must follow"—lies my objection to the logic of science. The arguments proceed from premises to conclusions, and end with the assumption "it therefore follows." But I say that, however carefully the argument be built up, even though apparently flawless, there is no such thing at present as "it must follow." Human ideas at present

naturally form a plan, and a balanced design;
they might be indicated by a geometrical figure,
an upright straight line in the centre, and
branching from that straight line curves on
either hand exactly equal to each other. In
drawing that is how we are taught, to balance
the outline or curves on one side with the
curves on the other. In nature and in fact
there is no such thing. The stem of a tree
represents the upright line, but the branches
do not balance; those on one side are larger
or longer than those on the other. Nothing
is straight, but all things curved, crooked, and
unequal.

The human body is the most remarkable
instance of inequality, lack of balance, and
want of plan. The exterior is beautiful in
its lines, but the two hands, the two feet, the
two sides of the face, the two sides of the
profile, are not precisely equal. The very
nails of the fingers are set ajar, as it were, to

the lines of the hand, and not quite straight.
Examination of the interior organs shows a
total absence of balance. The heart is not
in the centre, nor do the organs correspond
in any way. The viscera are wholly opposed
to plan. Coming, lastly, to the bones, these
have no humanity, as it were, of shape; they
are neither round nor square; the first sight
of them causes a sense of horror, so extra-
human are they in shape; there is no balance
of design in them. These are very brief
examples, but the whole universe, so far as it
can be investigated, is equally unequal. No
straight line runs through it, with balanced
curves each side.

Let this thought now be carried into the
realms of thought. The mind, or circle, or
sequence of ideas, acts, or thinks, or exists in
a balance, or what seems a balance to it. A
straight line of thought is set in the centre,
with equal branches each side, and with a

generally rounded outline. But this corre-
sponds to nothing in tangible fact. Hence I
think, by analogy, we may suppose that
neither does it correspond to the circle of
ideas which caused us and all things to be,
or, at all events, to the circle of ideas which
accurately understand us and all things.
There are other ideas altogether. From
standing face to face so long with the real
earth, the real sun, and the real sea, I am
firmly convinced that there is an immense
range of thought quite unknown to us yet.

The problem of my own existence also
convinces me that there is much more. The
questions are : Did my soul exist before my
body was formed? Or did it come into life
with my body, as a product, like a flame, of
combustion ? What will become of it after
death ? Will it simply go out like a flame
and become non-existent, or will it live for
ever in one or other mode ? To these ques-

tions I am unable to find any answer whatsoever. In our present range of ideas there
is no reply to them. I may have previously
existed; I may not have previously existed.
I may be a product of combustion; I may
exist on after physical life is suspended, or
I may not. No demonstration is possible.
But what I want to say is that the alternatives of extinction or immortality may not
be the only alternatives. There may be
something else, more wonderful than immortality, and far beyond and above that
idea. There may be something immeasurably superior to it. As our ideas have run
in circles for centuries, it is difficult to find
words to express the idea that there are
other ideas. For myself, though I cannot
fully express myself, I feel fully convinced
that there is a vast immensity of thought, of
existence, and of other things beyond even
immortal existence.

CHAPTER IX

In human affairs everything happens by chance—that is, in defiance of human ideas, and without any direction of an intelligence. A man bathes in a pool, a crocodile seizes and lacerates his flesh. If any one maintains that an intelligence directed that cruelty, I can only reply that his mind is under an illusion. A man is caught by a revolving shaft and torn to pieces, limb from limb. There is no directing intelligence in human affairs, no protection, and no assistance. Those who act uprightly are not rewarded, but they and their children often wander in the utmost indigence. Those who do evil are not always punished, but frequently flourish and have happy children. Rewards and punishments are purely human institutions, and if government be relaxed they entirely disappear. No intelligence whatever interferes in human affairs. There is a most senseless belief now prevalent that effort, and work, and cleverness, perseverance and industry, are invariably successful. Were this the case, every man would enjoy a competence, at least, and be free from the cares of money. This is an illusion almost equal to the superstition of a directing intelligence, which every fact and every consideration disproves.

How can I adequately express my contempt for the assertion that all things occur for the best, for a wise and beneficent end, and are ordered by a humane intelligence! It is the most utter falsehood and a crime against the human race. Even in my brief time I have been contemporary with events of the most horrible character; as when the mothers in the Balkans cast their own children from

the train to perish in the snow; as when the
Princess Alice foundered, and six hundred
human beings were smothered in foul water;
as when the hecatomb of two thousand
maidens were burned in the church at Sant-
iago; as when the miserable creatures tore at
the walls of the Vienna theatre. Consider only
the fates which overtake the little children.
Human suffering is so great, so endless, so
awful that I can hardly write of it. I could
not go into hospitals and face it, as some do,
lest my mind should be temporarily overcome.
The whole and the worst the worst pessimist
can say is far beneath the least particle of the
truth, so immense is the misery of man. It
is the duty of all rational beings to acknowledge the truth. There is not the least trace
of directing intelligence in human affairs.
This is a foundation of hope, because, if the
present condition of things were ordered by
a superior power, there would be no possi-

bility of improving it for the better in the spite of that power. Acknowledging that no such direction exists, all things become at once plastic to our will.

The credit given by the unthinking to the statement that all affairs are directed has been the bane of the world since the days of the Egyptian papyri and the origin of superstition. So long as men firmly believe that everything is fixed for them, so long is progress impossible. If you argue yourself into the belief that you cannot walk to a place, you cannot walk there. But if you start you can walk there easily. Any one who will consider the affairs of the world at large, and of the individual, will see that they do not proceed in the manner they would do for our own happiness if a man of humane breadth of view were placed at their head with unlimited power, such as is credited to the intelligence which does not exist. A man of intellect and humanity could cause everything to happen in an infinitely superior manner. Could one like the divine Julius—humane, generous, broadest of view, deep thinking—wield such power, certainly every human being would enjoy happiness.

But that which is thoughtlessly credited to a non-existent intelligence should really be claimed and exercised by the human race. It is ourselves who should direct our affairs, protecting ourselves from pain, assisting ourselves, succouring and rendering our lives happy. We must do for ourselves what superstition has hitherto supposed an intelligence to do for us. Nothing whatsoever is done for us. We are born naked, and not even protected by a shaggy covering. Nothing is done for us. The first and strongest command (using the word to convey the idea only) that nature, the universe, our own bodies give, is to do everything for ourselves.

The sea does not make boats for us, nor the earth of her own will build us hospitals. The injured lie bleeding, and no invisible power lifts them up. The maidens were scorched in the midst of their devotions, and their remains make a mound hundreds of yards long. The infants perished in the snow, and the ravens tore their limbs. Those in the theatre crushed each other to the death-agony. For how long, for how many thousand years, must the earth and the sea, and the fire and the air, utter these things and force them upon us before they are admitted in their full significance?

These things speak with a voice of thunder. From every human being whose body has been racked by pain; from every human being who has suffered from accident or disease; from every human being drowned, burned, or slain by negligence, there goes up a continually increasing cry louder than the thunder. An awe-inspiring cry dread to listen to, which no one dares listen to, against which ears are stopped by the wax of superstition and the wax of criminal selfishness :— These miseries are your doing, because you have mind and thought, and could have prevented them. You can prevent them in the future. You do not even try.

It is perfectly certain that all diseases without exception are preventible, or, if not so, that they can be so weakened as to do no harm. It is perfectly certain that all accidents are preventible; there is not one that does not arise from folly or negligence. All accidents are crimes. It is perfectly certain that all human beings are capable of physical happiness. It is absolutely incontrovertible that the ideal shape of the human being is attainable to the exclusion of deformities. It is incontrovertible that there is no necessity for any man to die but of old age, and that if

death cannot be prevented life can be prolonged far beyond the farthest now known.
It is incontrovertible that at the present time
no one ever dies of old age. Not one single
person ever dies of old age, or of natural
causes, for there is no such thing as a natural
cause of death. They die of disease or weakness which is the result of disease either in
themselves or in their ancestors. No such
thing as old age is known to us. We do
not even know what old age would be like,
because no one ever lives to it.

Our bodies are full of unsuspected flaws,
handed down it may be for thousands of
years, and it is of these that we die, and not
of natural decay. Till these are eliminated,
or as nearly eliminated as possible, we shall
never even know what true old age is like, nor
what the true natural limit of human life is.
The utmost limit now appears to be about
one hundred and five years, but as each person

who has got so far has died of weaknesses inherited through thousands of years, it is impossible to say to what number of years he
would have reached in a natural state. It
seems more than possible that true old age—
the slow and natural decay of the body apart
from inherited flaw—would be free from very
many, if not all, of the petty miseries which
now render extreme age a doubtful blessing.
If the limbs grew weaker they would not
totter; if the teeth dropped it would not be
till the last; if the eyes were less strong
they would not be quite dim; nor would the
mind lose its memory.

But now we see eyes become dim and
artificial aid needed in comparative youth,
and teeth drop out in mere childhood. Many
men and women lose teeth before they are
twenty. This simple fact is evidence enough
of inherited weakness or flaw. How could a
person who had lost teeth before twenty be

ever said to die of old age, though he died at a hundred and ten? Death is not a supernatural event; it is an event of the most materialistic .character, and may certainly be postponed, by the united efforts of the human race, to a period far more distant from the date of birth than has been the case during the historic period. The question has often been debated in my mind whether death is or is not wholly preventible; whether, if the entire human race were united in their efforts to eliminate causes of decay, death might not also be altogether eliminated.

If we consider ourselves by the analogy of animals, trees, and other living creatures, the reply is that, however postponed, in long process of time the tissues must wither. Suppose an ideal man, free from inherited flaw, then though his age might be prolonged to several centuries, in the end the natural body must wear out. That is true so far.

But it so happens that the analogy is not just, and therefore the conclusions it points to are not tenable.

Man is altogether different from every other animal, every other living creature known. He is different in body. In his purely natural state—in his true natural state —he is immeasurably stronger. No animal approaches to the physical perfection of which a man is capable. He can weary the strongest horse, he can outrun the swiftest stag, he can bear extremes of heat and cold, hunger and thirst, which would exterminate every known living thing. Merely in bodily strength he is superior to all. The stories of antiquity, which were deemed fables, may be fables historically, but search has shown that they are not intrinsically fables. Man of flesh and blood is capable of all that Ajax, all that Hercules did. Feats in modern days have surpassed these, as when Webb swam the

Channel; mythology contains nothing equal to that. The difference does not end here. Animals think to a certain extent, but if their conceptions be ever so clever, not having hands they cannot execute them.

I myself maintain that the mind of man is practically infinite. It can understand anything brought before it. It has not the power of its own motion to bring everything before it, but when anything is brought it is understood. It is like sitting in a room with one window; you cannot compel everything to pass the window, but whatever does pass is seen. It is like a magnifying glass, which magnifies and explains everything brought into its focus. The mind of man is infinite. Beyond this, man has a soul. I do not use this word in the common sense which circumstances have given to it. I use it as the only term to express that inner consciousness which aspires. These brief reasons show that

the analogy is imperfect, and that therefore,
although an ideal animal—a horse, a dog, a
lion—must die, it does not follow that an
ideal man must.   He has a body possessed of
exceptional recuperative powers, which, under
proper conditions, continually repairs itself.
He has a mind by which he can select re-
medies, and select his course and carefully
restore the waste of tissue.   He has a soul,
as yet, it seems to me, lying in abeyance, by
the aid of which he may yet discover things
now deemed supernatural.

Considering these things I am obliged by
facts and incontrovertible argument to conclude that death is not inevitable to the ideal
man.   He is shaped for a species of physical
immortality.   The beauty of form of the ideal
human being indicates immortality—the con-
tour, the curve, the outline answer to the idea
of life.   In the course of ages united effort
long continued may eliminate those causes of

decay which have grown up in ages past, and after that has been done advance farther and improve the natural state. As a river brings down suspended particles of sand, and depositing them at its mouth forms a delta and a new country; as the air and the rain and the heat of the sun desiccate the rocks and slowly wear down mountains into sand, so the united action of the human race, continued through centuries, may build up the ideal man and woman. Each individual labouring in his day through geological time in front must produce an effect. The instance of Sparta, where so much was done in a few centuries, is almost proof of it.

The truth is, we die through our ancestors; we are murdered by our ancestors. Their dead hands stretch forth from the tomb and drag us down to their mouldering bones. We in our turn are now at this moment preparing death for our unborn posterity. This day those that die do not die in the sense of old age, they are slain. Nothing has been accumulated for our benefit in ages past. All the labour and the toil of so many millions continued through such vistas of time, down to those millions who at this hour are rushing to and fro in London, has accumulated nothing for us. Nothing for our good. The only things that have been stored up have been for our evil and destruction, diseases and weaknesses crossed and cultivated and rendered almost part and parcel of our very bones. Now let us begin to roll back the tide of death, and to set our faces steadily to a future of life. It should be the sacred and sworn duty of every one, once at least during lifetime, to do something in person towards this end. It would be a delight and pleasure to me to do something every day, were it ever so minute. To reflect that another human being, if at a distance of ten thousand years from the year 1883, would enjoy one hour's more life, in the sense of fulness of life, in consequence of anything I had done in my little span, would be to me a peace of soul.

CHAPTER X

United effort through geological time in front is but the beginning of an idea. I am convinced that much more can be done, and that the length of time may be almost immeasurably shortened. The general principles that are now in operation are of the simplest and most elementary character, yet they have already made considerable difference. I am not content with these. There must be much more—there must be things which are at present unknown by whose aid advance may be made. Research proceeds upon the same old lines and runs in the ancient grooves. Further, it is restricted by the ultra-practical views which are alone deemed reasonable. But there should be no limit placed on the mind. The purely ideal is as worthy of pursuit as the practical, and the mind is not to be pinned to dogmas of science any more than to dogmas of superstition. Most injurious of all is the continuous circling on the same path, and it is from this that I wish to free my mind.

The pursuit of theory—the organon of pure thought—has led incidentally to great discoveries, and for myself I am convinced it is of the highest value. The process of experiment has produced much, and has applied what was previously found. Empiricism is worthy of careful re-working out, for it is a fact that most things are more or less empirical, especially in medicine. Denial may be given to this statement, nevertheless it is true, and I have had practical exemplification of it in my own experience. Observation is perhaps more

powerful an organon than either experiment
or empiricism. If the eye is always watching, and the mind on the alert, ultimately
chance supplies the solution.

The difficulties I have encountered have
generally been solved by chance in this way.
When I took an interest in archæological
matters—an interest long since extinct—I
considered that a part of an army known to
have marched in a certain direction during
the Civil War must have visited a town in
which I was interested. But I exhausted
every mode of research in vain; there was
no evidence of it. If the knowledge had
ever existed it had dropped again. Some
years afterwards, when my interest had ceased,
and I had put such inquiries for ever aside
(being useless, like the Egyptian papyri), I
was reading in the British Museum. Presently I returned my book to the shelf, and
then slowly walked along the curving wall

lined with volumes, looking to see if I could light on anything to amuse me. I took out a volume for a glance; it opened of itself at a certain page, and there was the information I had so long sought—a reprint of an old pamphlet describing the visit of the army to the town in the Civil War. So chance answered the question in the course of time.

And. I think that, seeing how great a part chance plays in human affairs, it is essential that study should be made of chance; it seems to me that an organon might be deduced from chance as much as from experiment. Then there is the inner consciousness—the psyche—that has never yet been brought to bear upon life and its questions. Besides which there is a super-sensuous reason. Often I have argued with myself that such and such a course was the right one to follow, while in the intervals of thinking about it an undercurrent of unconscious impulse has desired me to do the reverse or to remain inactive. Sometimes it has happened that the supersensuous reasoning has been correct, and the most faultless argument wrong. I presume this supersensuous reasoning, proceeding independently in the mind, arises from perceptions too delicate for analysis. From these considerations alone I am convinced that, by the aid of ideas yet to be discovered, the geological time in front may be immeasurably shortened. These modes of research are not all. The psyche —the soul in me—tells me that there is much more, that these are merely beginnings of the crudest kind.

I fully recognise the practical difficulty arising from the ingrained, hereditary, and unconscious selfishness which began before history, and has been crossed and cultivated for twelve thousand years since. This renders me less sanguine of united effort through geological time ahead, unless some idea can be formed to give a stronger impulse even than selfishness, or unless the selfishness can be utilised. The complacency with which the mass of people go about their daily task, absolutely indifferent to all other considerations, is appalling in its concentrated stolidity. They do not intend wrong — they intend rightly: in truth, they work against the entire human race. So wedded and so confirmed is the world in its narrow groove of self, so stolid and so complacent under the immense weight of misery, so callous to its own possibilities, and so grown to its chains, that I almost despair to see it awakened. Cemeteries are often placed on hillsides, and the white stones are visible far off. If the whole of the dead in a hillside cemetery were called up alive from their tombs, and walked forth down into the valley, it would not rouse the mass of people from

the dense pyramid of stolidity which presses
on them.

There would be gaping and marvelling
and rushing about, and what then? In a
week or two the ploughman would settle
down to his plough, the carpenter to his
bench, the smith to his anvil, the merchant
to his money, and the dead come to life
would be utterly forgotten. No matter in
what manner the possibilities of human life
are put before the world, the crowd continues as stolid as before. Therefore nothing
hitherto done, or suggested, or thought of,
is of much avail; but this fact in no degree
stays me from the search. On the contrary,
the less there has been accomplished the
more anxious I am; the truth it teaches is
that the mind must be lifted out of its old
grooves before anything will be certainly
begun. Erase the past from the mind—
stand face to face with the real now—and

work out all anew. Call the soul to our assistance; the soul tells me that outside all the ideas that have yet occurred there are others, whole circles of others.

I remember a cameo of Augustus Cæsar— the head of the emperor is graven in delicate lines, and shows the most exquisite proportions. It is a balanced head, a head adjusted to the calmest intellect. That head when it was living contained a circle of ideas, the largest, the widest, the most profound current in his time. All that philosophy had taught, all that practice, experiment, and empiricism had discovered, was familiar to him. There was no knowledge in the ancient world but what was accessible to the Emperor of Rome. Now at this day there are amongst us heads as finely proportioned as that cut out in the cameo. Though these living men do not possess arbitrary power, the advantages of arbitrary power—as far as knowledge is concerned—are secured to them by education, by the printing-press, and the facilities of our era. It is reasonable to imagine a head of our time filled with the largest, the widest, the most profound ideas current in the age. Augustus Cæsar, however great his intellect, could not in that balanced head have possessed the ideas familiar enough to the living head of this day. As we have a circle of ideas unknown to Augustus Cæsar, so I argue there are whole circles of ideas unknown to us. It is these that I am so earnestly desirous of discovering.

For nothing has as yet been of any value, however good its intent. There is no virtue, or reputed virtue, which has not been rigidly pursued, and things have remained as before. Men and women have practised self-denial, and to what end? They have compelled themselves to suffer hunger and thirst; in vain. They have clothed themselves in sackcloth and lacerated the flesh. They have mutilated themselves. Some have been scrupulous to bathe, and some have been scrupulous to cake their bodies with the foulness of years. Many have devoted their lives to assist others in sickness or poverty. Chastity has been faithfully observed, chastity both of body and mind. Self-examination has been pursued till it ended in a species of sacred insanity, and all these have been of no more value than the tortures undergone by the Indian mendicant who hangs himself up by a hook through his back. All these are pure folly.

Asceticism has not improved the form, or the physical well-being, or the heart of any human being. On the contrary, the hetaira is often the warmest hearted and the most generous. Casuistry and self-examination are perhaps the most injurious of all the virtues, utterly destroying independence of mind. Self-denial has had no result, and all the self-torture of centuries has been thrown away. Lives spent in doing good have been lives nobly wasted. Everything is in vain. The circle of ideas we possess is too limited to aid us. We need ideas as far outside our circle as ours are outside those that were pondered over by Augustus Cæsar.

The most extraordinary spectacle, as it seems to me, is the vast expenditure of labour and time wasted in obtaining mere subsistence. As a man, in his lifetime, works hard and saves money, that his children may be free from the cares of penury and may at least have sufficient to eat, drink, clothe, and roof them, so the generations that preceded us might, had they so chosen, have provided for our subsistence. The labour and time of ten generations, properly directed, would sustain a hundred generations succeeding to them, and that, too, with so little self-denial on the part of the providers as to be scarcely felt. So men now, in this generation, ought clearly to be laying up a store, or, what is still more powerful, arranging and organising that the generations which follow may enjoy comparative freedom from useless labour. Instead of which, with transcendent improvidence, the world works only for to-day, as the world worked twelve thousand years ago, and our children's children will still have to toil and slave for the bare necessities of life. This is, indeed, an extraordinary spectacle.

That twelve thousand written years should have elapsed, and the human race—able to reason and to think, and easily capable of combination in immense armies for its own destruction — should still live from hand to mouth, like cattle and sheep, like the animals of the field and the birds of the woods; that there should not even be roofs to cover the children born, unless those children labour and expend their time to pay for them; that there should not be clothes, unless, again, time and labour are expended to procure them; that there should not be even food for the children of the human race, except they labour as their fathers did twelve thousand years ago; that even water should scarce be accessible to them, unless paid for by labour! In twelve thousand written years the world has not yet built itself a House, nor filled a Granary, nor organised itself for its own comfort. It is so marvellous I cannot express the wonder with which it fills me. And more wonderful still, if that could be, there are people so infatuated, or, rather, so limited of view, that they glory in this state of things, declaring that work is the main object of man's existence — work for sub-sistence—and glorying in their wasted time. To argue with such is impossible; to leave them is the only resource.

This our earth this day produces sufficient for our existence. This our earth produces not only a sufficiency, but a superabundance, and pours a cornucopia of good things down upon us. Further, it produces sufficient for stores and granaries to be filled to the roof-tree for years ahead. I verily believe that the earth in one year produces enough food to last for thirty. Why, then, have we not enough? Why do people die of starvation, or lead a miserable existence on the verge of it? Why have millions upon millions to toil from morning to evening just to gain a mere crust of bread? Because of the absolute lack of organisation by which such labour should produce its effect, the absolute lack of distribution, the absolute lack even of the very idea that such things are possible. Nay, even to mention such things, to say that they are possible, is criminal with many. Madness could hardly go farther.

That selfishness has all to do with it I entirely deny. The human race for ages upon ages has been enslaved by ignorance and by interested persons whose object it has been to confine the minds of men, thereby doing more injury than if with infected hands they purposely imposed disease on the heads of the people. Almost worse than these, and at the present day as injurious, are those persons incessantly declaring, teaching, and impressing upon all that to work is man's highest condition. This falsehood is the interested superstition of an age infatuated with money, which having accumulated it cannot even expend it in pageantry. It is a falsehood propagated for the doubtful benefit of two or three out of ten thousand. It is the lie of a morality founded on money only, and utterly outside and having no association whatever with the human being in itself. Many superstitions have been got rid of in these days; time it is that this, the last and worst, were eradicated.

At this hour, out of thirty-four millions who inhabit this country, two-thirds — say twenty-two millions—live within thirty years of that abominable institution the poorhouse. That any human being should dare to apply to another the epithet "pauper" is, to me, the greatest, the vilest, the most unpardonable crime that could be committed. Each human being, by mere birth, has a birthright in this earth and all its productions; and if they do not receive it, then it is they who are injured, and it is not the "pauper"—oh, inexpressibly wicked word!—it is the well-to-do, who are the criminal classes. It matters

not in the least if the poor be improvident,
or drunken, or evil in any way. Food and
drink, roof and clothes, are the inalienable
right of every child born into the light. If
the world does not provide it freely—not as
a grudging gift but as a right, as a son of
the house sits down to breakfast — then is
the world mad. But the world is not mad,
only in ignorance—an interested ignorance,
kept up by strenuous exertions, from which
infernal darkness it will, in course of time,
emerge, marvelling at the past as a man
wonders at and glories in the light who has
escaped from blindness.

CHAPTER XI

THIS our earth produces not only a sufficiency and a superabundance, but in one year pours a cornucopia of good things forth, enough to fill us all for many years in succession. The only reason we do not enjoy it is the want of rational organisation. I know, of course, and all who think know, that some labour or supervision will be always necessary, since the plough must travel the furrow and the seed must be sown; but I maintain that a tenth, nay, a hundredth, part of the labour and slavery now gone through will be sufficient, and that in the course of time, as organisation perfects itself and discoveries advance, even that part will diminish. For the rise and fall of the tides alone furnish forth sufficient power to do automatically all the labour that is done on the earth. Is ideal man, then, to be idle? I answer that, if so, I see no wrong, but a great good. I deny alto-gether that idleness is an evil, or that it produces evil, and I am well aware why the interested are so bitter against idleness — namely, because it gives time for thought, and if men had time to think their reign would come to an end. Idleness—that is, the absence of the necessity to work for subsistence—is a great good.

I hope succeeding generations will be able to be idle. I hope that nine-tenths of their time will be leisure time; that they may enjoy their days, and the earth, and the beauty of this beautiful world; that they may rest by the sea and dream; that they may dance and sing, and eat and drink. I will work towards that end with all my heart. If employment they must have—and the restlessness of the mind will insure that some will be followed—then they will find scope enough in the perfection of their physical frames, in the expansion of the mind, and in the enlargement of the soul. They shall not work for bread, but for their souls. I am willing to divide and share all I shall ever have for this purpose, though I think that the end will rather be gained by organisation than by sharing alone.

In these material things, too, I think that we require another circle of ideas, and I believe that such ideas are possible, and, in a manner of speaking, exist. Let me exhort every one to do their utmost to think outside and beyond our present circle of ideas. For every idea gained is a hundred years of slavery remitted. Even with the idea of organisation which promises most I am not satisfied, but endeavour to get beyond and outside it, so that the time now necessary may be shortened. Besides which, I see that many of our difficulties arise from obscure and remote causes—obscure like the shape of bones, for whose strange curves there is no familiar term. We must endeavour to understand the crookedness and unfamiliar curves of the conditions of life. Beyond that still there are other ideas. Never, never rest contented with any circle of ideas, but always be certain that a wider one is still possible. For my thought is like a hyperbola that continually widens ascending.

For grief there is no known consolation. It is useless to fill our hearts with bubbles. A loved one gone is gone, and as to the future—even if there is a future—it is unknown. To assure ourselves otherwise is to soothe the mind with illusions; the bitterness of it is inconsolable. The sentiments of trust chipped out on tombstones are touching instances of the innate goodness of the human heart, which naturally longs for good, and sighs itself to sleep in the hope that, if parted, the parting is for the benefit of those that are gone. But these inscriptions are also awful instances of the deep intellectual darkness which presses still on the minds of men. The least thought erases them. There is no consolation. There is no relief. There is no hope certain; the whole system is a mere illusion. I, who hope so much, and am so rapt up in the soul, know full well that there is no certainty.

The tomb cries aloud to us—its dead silence presses on the drum of the ear like thunder, saying, Look at this, and erase your illusions; now know the extreme value of human life; reflect on this and strew human life with flowers; save every hour for the sunshine; let your labour be so ordered that in future times the loved ones may dwell longer with those who love them; open your minds; exalt your souls; widen the sympathies of your hearts; face the things that are now as you will face the reality of death; make joy real now to those you love, and help forward the joy of those yet to be born. Let these facts force the mind and the soul to the increase of thought, and the consequent remission of misery; so that those whose time it is to die may have enjoyed all that is possible in life. Lift up your mind and see now in this bitterness of parting, in this absence of certainty, the fact that there is no directing intelligence; remember that this death is not of old age, which no one living in the world has ever seen; remember that old age is possible, and perhaps even more than old age; and beyond these earthly things—what? None know. But let us, turning away from the illusion of a directing intelligence, look earnestly for something better than a god, seek for something higher than prayer, and lift our souls to be with the more than immortal now.

A river runs itself clear during the night, and in sleep thought becomes pellucid. All the hurrying to and fro, the unrest and stress, the agitation and confusion subside. Like a sweet pure spring, thought pours forth to meet the light, and is illumined to its depths. The dawn at my window ever causes a desire for larger thought, the recognition of the light at the moment of waking kindles afresh the wish for a broad day of the mind. There is a certainty that there are yet ideas further, and greater—that there is still a limitless beyond. I know at that moment that there is no limit to the things that may be yet in material and tangible shape besides the immaterial perceptions of the soul. The dim white light of the dawn speaks it. This prophet which has come with its wonders to the bedside of every human being for so many thousands of years faces me once again with the upheld finger of light. Where is the limit to that physical sign?

From space to the sky, from the sky to the hills, and the sea; to every blade of grass, to every leaf, to the smallest insect, to the million waves of ocean. Yet this earth itself appears but a mote in that sunbeam by which we are conscious of one narrow streak in the abyss. A beam crosses my silent chamber from the window, and atoms are visible in it; a beam slants between the fir-trees, and particles rise and fall within, and cross it while the air each side seems void. Through the heavens a beam slants, and we are aware of the star-stratum in which our earth moves. But what may be without that stratum? Certainly it is not a void. This light tells us much, but I think in the course of time yet more delicate and subtle mediums than light may be found, and through these we shall see into the shadows of the sky. When will it be possible to be certain that the capacity of a single atom has been exhausted? At any moment some fortunate incident may reveal a fresh power. One by one the powers of light have been unfolded.

After thousands of years the telescope opened the stars, the prism analysed the substance of the sun, the microscope showed the minute structure of the rocks and the tissues of living bodies. The winged men on the Assyrian bas-reliefs, the gods of the Nile, the chariot-borne immortals of Olympus, not the greatest of imagined beings ever possessed in fancied attributes one-tenth the power of light. As the swallows twitter, the dim white finger appears at my window full of wonders, such as all the wise men in twelve thousand precedent years never even hoped to conceive. But this is not all— light is not all; light conceals more than it reveals; light is the darkest shadow of the sky; besides light there are many other mediums yet to be explored. For thousands of years the sunbeams poured on the earth, full as now of messages, and light is not a hidden thing to be searched out with difficulty. Full in the faces of men the rays came with their intelligence from the sun when the papyri were painted beside the ancient Nile, but they were not understood.

This hour, rays or undulations of more subtle mediums are doubtless pouring on us over the wide earth, unrecognised, and full of messages and intelligence from the unseen. Of these we are this day as ignorant as those who painted the papyri were of light. There is an infinity of knowledge yet to be known, and beyond that an infinity of thought. No mental instrument even has yet been invented by which researches can be carried direct to the object. Whatever has been found has been discovered by fortunate accident; in looking for one thing another has been chanced on. A reasoning process has yet to be invented by which to go straight to the desired end. For now the slightest particle is enough to throw the search aside, and the most minute circumstance sufficient to conceal obvious and brilliantly shining truths. One summer evening sitting by my window I watched for the first star to appear, knowing the position of the brightest in the southern sky. The dusk came on, grew deeper, but the star did not shine. By-and-by, other stars less bright appeared, so that it could not be the sunset which obscured the expected one. Finally, I considered that I must have mistaken its position, when suddenly a puff of air blew through the branch of a pear-tree which overhung the window, a leaf moved, and there was the star behind the leaf.

At present the endeavour to make discoveries is like gazing at the sky up through the boughs of an oak. Here a beautiful star shines clearly; here a constellation is hidden by a branch; a universe by a leaf. Some mental instrument or organon is required to enable us to distinguish between the leaf which may be removed and a real void; when to cease to look in one direction, and to work in another. Many men of broad brow and great intellect lived in the days of ancient Greece, but for lack of the accident of a lens, and of knowing the way to use a prism, they could but conjecture imperfectly. I am in exactly the position they were when I look beyond light. Outside my present knowledge I am exactly in their condition. I feel that there are infinities to be known, but they are hidden by a leaf. If any one says to himself that the telescope, and the microscope, the prism, and other discoveries have made all plain, then he is in the attitude of those ancient priests who worshipped the scarabæus or beetle. So, too, it is with thought; outside our present circle of ideas I believe there is an infinity of idea. All this that has been effected with light has been done by bits of glass—mere bits of shaped glass, quickly broken, and made of flint, so that by the rude flint our subtlest ideas are gained. Could we employ the ocean as a lens, and force truth from the sky, even then I think there would be much more beyond.

Natural things are known to us only under two conditions—matter and force, or matter and motion. A third, a fourth, a fifth —no one can say how many conditions—may exist in the ultra-stellar space, and such other conditions may equally exist about us now unsuspected. Something which is neither matter nor force is difficult to conceive, yet, I think, it is certain that there are other conditions. When the mind succeeds in entering on a wider series, or circle of ideas, other conditions would appear natural enough. In this effort upwards I claim the assistance of the soul—the mind of the mind. The eye sees, the mind deliberates on what it sees, the soul understands the operation of the mind. Before a bridge is built, or a structure erected, or an interoceanic canal made, there must be a plan, and before a plan the thought in the mind. So that it is correct to say the mind bores tunnels through the mountains, bridges the rivers, and constructs the engines which are the pride of the world.

This is a wonderful tool, but it is capable of work yet more wonderful in the exploration of the heavens. Now the soul is the mind of the mind. It can build and construct and look beyond and penetrate space, and create. It is the keenest, the sharpest tool possessed by man. But what would be said if a carpenter about to commence a piece of work examined his tools and deliberately cast away that with the finest edge? Such is the conduct of those who reject the inner mind or psyche altogether. So great is the value of the soul that it seems to me, if the soul lived and received its aspirations it would not matter if the material universe melted away as snow. Many turn aside the instant the soul is mentioned, and I sympathise with them in one sense; they fear lest, if they acknowledge it, they will be fettered by mediæval conditions. My contention is that the restrictions of the mediæval era should entirely be cast into oblivion, but the soul recognised and employed. Instead of slurring over the soul, I desire to see it at its highest perfection.

CHAPTER XII

SUBTLE as the mind is, it can effect little without knowledge. It cannot construct a bridge, or a building, or make a canal, or work a problem in algebra, unless it is provided with information. This is obvious, and yet some say, What can you effect by the soul? I reply because it has had no employment. Mediæval conditions kept it in slumber: science refuses to accept it. We are taught to employ our minds, and furnished with materials. The mind has its logic and exercise of geometry, and thus assisted brings a great force to the solution of problems. The soul remains untaught, and can effect little.

I consider that the highest purpose of

study is the education of the soul or psyche. It is said that there is no proof of the existence of the soul, but, arguing on the same grounds, there is no proof of the existence of the mind, which is not a tangible thing. For myself, I feel convinced that there is a soul, a mind of the mind—and that it really exists. Now, glancing at the state of wild and uneducated men, it is evident that they work with their hands and make various things almost instinctively. But when they arrive at the idea of mind, and say to themselves, I possess a mind, then they think and proceed farther, forming designs and constructions both tangible and mental.

Next then, when we say, I have a soul, we can proceed to shape things yet further, and to see deeper, and penetrate the mystery. By denying the existence and the power of the soul—refusing to employ it—we should go back more than twelve thousand written

years of human history. But instead of this,
I contend, we should endeavour to go forward, and to discover a fourth Idea, and after
that a fifth, and onwards continually.

I will not permit myself to be taken
captive by observing physical phenomena, as
many evidently are. Some gases are mingled
and produce a liquid; certainly it is worth
careful investigation, but it is no more than
the revolution of a wheel, which is so often
seen that it excites no surprise, though, in
truth, as wonderful. So is all motion, and so
is a grain of sand; there is nothing that is
not wonderful; as, for instance, the fact of
the existence of things at all. But the intense concentration of the mind on mechanical effects appears often to render it
incapable of perceiving anything that is not
mechanical. Some compounds are observed
to precipitate crystals, all of which contain
known angles. Thence it is argued that all

is mechanical, and that action occurs in set ways only. There is a tendency to lay it down as an infallible law that because we see these things therefore everything else that exists in space must be or move exactly in the same manner. But I do not think that because crystals are precipitated with fixed angles therefore the whole universe is necessarily mechanical. I think there are things exempt from mechanical rules. The restriction of thought to purely mechanical grooves blocks progress in the same way as the restrictions of mediæval superstition. Let the mind think, dream, imagine: let it have perfect freedom. To shut out the soul is to put us back more than twelve thousand years.

Just as outside light, and the knowledge gained from light, there are, I think, other mediums from which, in times to come, intelligence will be obtained, so outside the mental and the spiritual ideas we now possess I believe there exists a whole circle of ideas. In the conception of the idea that there are others, I lay claim to another idea.

The mind is infinite and able to understand everything that is brought before it; there is no limit to its understanding. The limit is in the littleness of the things and the, narrowness of the ideas which have been put for it to consider. For the philosophies of old time past and the discoveries of modern research are as nothing to it. They do not fill it. When they have been read, the mind passes on, and asks for more. The utmost of them, the whole together, make a mere nothing. These things have been gathered together by immense labour, labour so great that it is a weariness to think of it; but yet, when all is summed up and written, the mind receives it all as easily as the hand picks flowers. It is like one sentence—read and gone.

The mind requires more, and more, and more. It is so strong that all that can be put before it is devoured in a moment. Left to itself it will not be satisfied with an invisible idol any more than with a wooden one. An idol whose attributes are omnipresence, omnipotence, and so on, is no greater than light or electricity, which are present everywhere and all-powerful, and from which perhaps the thought arose. Prayer which receives no reply must be pronounced in vain. The mind goes on and requires more than these, something higher than prayer, something higher than a god.

I have been obliged to write these things by an irresistible impulse which has worked in me since early youth. They have not been written for the sake of argument, still less for any thought of profit, rather indeed the reverse. They have been forced from me by earnestness of heart, and they express my most serious convictions. For seventeen years they have been lying in my mind, continually thought of and pondered over. I was not more than eighteen when an inner and esoteric meaning began to come to me from all the visible universe, and indefinable aspirations filled me. I found them in the grass fields, under the trees, on the hill-tops, at sunrise, and in the night. There was a deeper meaning everywhere. The sun burned with it, the broad front of morning beamed with it; a deep feeling entered me while gazing at the sky in the azure noon, and in the star-lit evening.

I was sensitive to all things, to the earth under, and the star-hollow round about; to the least blade of grass, to the largest oak. They seemed like exterior nerves and veins

for the conveyance of feeling to me. Sometimes a very ecstasy of exquisite enjoyment
of the entire visible universe filled me. I
was aware that in reality the feeling and
the thought were in me, and not in the
earth or sun; yet I was more conscious of
it when in company with these. A visit
to the sea increased the strength of the
original impulse. I began to make efforts
to express these thoughts in writing, but
could not succeed to my own liking. Time
went on, and harder experiences, and the
pressure of labour came, but in no degree
abated the fire of first thought. Again and
again I made resolutions that I would write
it, in some way or other, and as often
failed. I could express any other idea with
ease, but not this. Once especially I remember, in a short interval of distasteful
labour, walking away to a spot by a brook

which skirts an ancient Roman wall, and there trying to determine and really commence to work. Again I failed. More time, more changes, and still the same thought running beneath everything. At last, in 1880, in the old castle of Pevensey, under happy circumstances, once more I resolved, and actually did write down a few notes. Even then I could not go on, but I kept the notes (I had destroyed all former beginnings), and in the end, two years afterwards, commenced this book.

After all this time and thought it is only a fragment, and a fragment scarcely hewn. Had I not made it personal I could scarcely have put it into any shape at all. But I felt that I could no longer delay, and that it must be done, however imperfectly. I am only too conscious of its imperfections, for I have as it were seventeen years of consciousness of my own inability to express this the idea of my life. I can only say that many of these short sentences are the result of long-continued thought. One of the greatest difficulties I have encountered is the lack of words to express ideas. By the word soul, or psyche, I mean that inner consciousness which aspires. By prayer I do not mean a request for anything preferred to a deity; I mean intense soul-emotion, intense aspiration. The word immortal is very inconvenient, and yet there is no other to convey the idea of soul-life. Even these definitions are deficient, and I must leave my book as a whole to give its own meaning to its words.

Time has gone on, and still, after so much pondering, I feel that I know nothing, that I have not yet begun; I have only just commenced to realise the immensity of thought which lies outside the knowledge of the senses. Still, on the hills and by the sea-shore, I seek and pray deeper than ever. The sun burns southwards over the sea and before the wave runs its shadow, constantly slipping on the advancing slope till it curls and covers its dark image at the shore. Over the rim of the horizon waves are flowing as high and wide as those that break upon the beach. These that come to me and beat the trembling shore are like the thoughts that have been known so long; like the ancient, iterated, and reiterated thoughts that have broken on the strand of mind for thousands of years. Beyond and over the horizon I feel that there are other waves of ideas unknown to me, flowing as the stream of ocean flows. Knowledge of facts is limit-less: they lie at my feet innumerable like the countless pebbles; knowledge of thought so circumscribed! Ever the same thoughts come that have been written down centuries and centuries.

Let me launch forth and sail over the rim of the sea yonder, and when another rim arises over that, and again and onwards into an ever-widening ocean of idea and life. For with all the strength of the wave, and its succeeding wave, the depth and race of the tide, the clear definition of the sky; with all the subtle power of the great sea, there rises an equal desire. Give me life strong and full as the brimming ocean; give me thoughts wide as its plain; give me a soul beyond these. Sweet is the bitter sea by the shore where the faint blue pebbles are lapped by the green-grey wave, where the wind-quivering foam is loth to leave the lashed stone. Sweet is the bitter sea, and the clear green in which the gaze seeks the soul, looking through the glass into itself. The sea thinks for me as I listen and ponder; the sea thinks, and every boom of the wave repeats my prayer.

Sometimes I stay on the wet sands as the tide rises, listening to the rush of the lines of foam in layer upon layer; the wash swells and circles about my feet, I lave my hands in it, I lift a little in my hollowed palm, I take the life of the sea to me. My soul rising to the immensity utters its desire-prayer with all the strength of the sea. Or, again, the full stream of ocean beats upon the shore, and the rich wind feeds the heart, the sun burns brightly; the sense of soul-life burns in me like a torch.

Leaving the shore I walk among the trees; a cloud passes, and the sweet short rain comes mingled with sunbeams and flower-scented air. The finches sing among the fresh green leaves of the beeches. Beautiful it is, in summer days, to see the wheat wave, and the long grass foam-flecked of flower yield and return to the wind. My soul of itself always desires; these are to it as fresh food. I have found in the hills another valley grooved in prehistoric times, where, climbing to the top of the hollow, I can see the sea. Down in the hollow I look up; the sky stretches over, the sun burns as it seems but just above the hill, and the wind sweeps onward. As the sky extends beyond the valley, so I know that there are ideas beyond the valley of my thought; I know that there is something infinitely higher than deity. The great sun burning in the sky, the sea, the firm earth, all the stars of night are feeble—all, all the cosmos is feeble; it is not strong enough to utter my prayer-desire. My soul cannot reach to its full desire of prayer. I need no earth, or sea, or sun to think my thought. If my thought-part—the psyche—were entirely separated from the body, and from the earth, I should of myself desire the same. In itself my soul desires; my existence, my soul-existence is in itself my prayer, and so long as it exists so long will it pray that I may have the fullest soul-life.

THE END

PRINTED IN GREAT BRITAIN BY NEILL AND CO., LTD., EDINBURGH.

Trieste

Trieste Publishing has a massive catalogue of classic book titles. Our aim is to provide readers with the highest quality reproductions of fiction and non-fiction literature that has stood the test of time. The many thousands of books in our collection have been sourced from libraries and private collections around the world.

The titles that Trieste Publishing has chosen to be part of the collection have been scanned to simulate the original. Our readers see the books the same way that their first readers did decades or a hundred or more years ago. Books from that period are often spoiled by imperfections that did not exist in the original. Imperfections could be in the form of blurred text, photographs, or missing pages. It is highly unlikely that this would occur with one of our books. Our extensive quality control ensures that the readers of Trieste Publishing's books will be delighted with their purchase. Our staff has thoroughly reviewed every page of all the books in the collection, repairing, or if necessary, rejecting titles that are not of the highest quality. This process ensures that the reader of one of Trieste Publishing's titles receives a volume that faithfully reproduces the original, and to the maximum degree possible, gives them the experience of owning the original work.

We pride ourselves on not only creating a pathway to an extensive reservoir of books of the finest quality, but also providing value to every one of our readers. Generally, Trieste books are purchased singly - on demand, however they may also be purchased in bulk. Readers interested in bulk purchases are invited to contact us directly to enquire about our tailored bulk rates. Email: customerservice@triestepublishing.com

You May Also Like

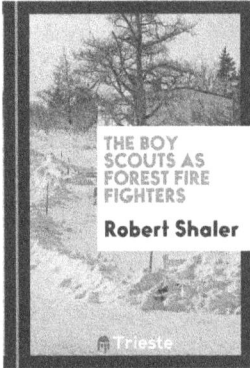

The Boy Scouts as Forest Fire Fighters

Robert Shaler

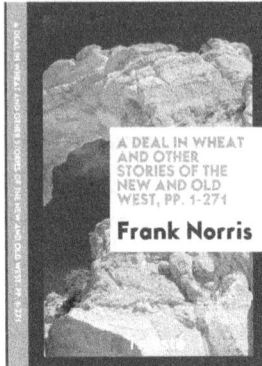

ISBN: 9781760579555
Paperback: 172 pages
Dimensions: 6.14 x 0.37 x 9.21 inches
Language: eng

A Deal in Wheat and Other Stories of the New and Old West, pp. 1-271

Frank Norris

ISBN: 9781760574345
Paperback: 298 pages
Dimensions: 6.0 x 0.62 x 9.0 inches
Language: eng

www.triestepublishing.com

You May Also Like

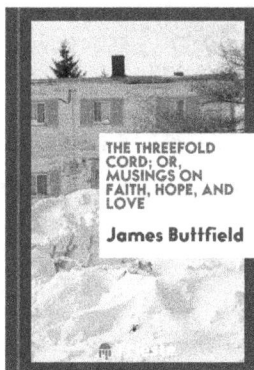

The Threefold Cord; Or, Musings on Faith, Hope, and Love

James Buttfield

ISBN: 9781760579548
Paperback: 160 pages
Dimensions: 6.14 x 0.34 x 9.21 inches
Language: eng

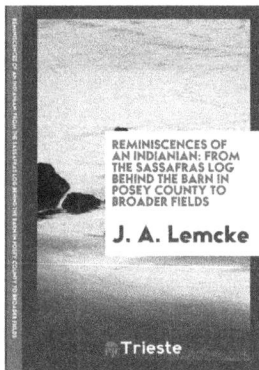

Reminiscences of an Indianian: From the Sassafras Log behind the Barn in Posey County to Broader Fields

J. A. Lemcke

ISBN: 9781760571467
Paperback: 242 pages
Dimensions: 6.14 x 0.51 x 9.21 inches
Language: eng

You May Also Like

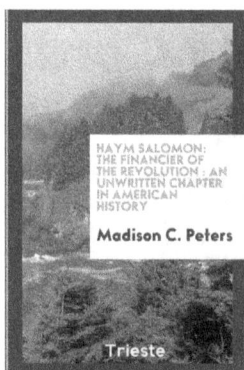

Haym Salomon: The Financier of the Revolution : an Unwritten Chapter in American History

Madison C. Peters

ISBN: 9781760570170
Paperback: 56 pages
Dimensions: 6.14 x 0.12 x 9.21 inches
Language: eng

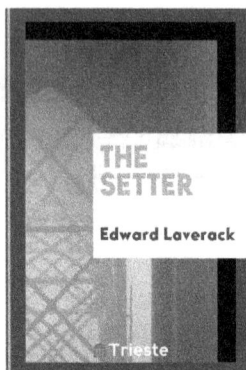

The setter

Edward Laverack

ISBN: 9781760570309
Paperback: 90 pages
Dimensions: 6.14 x 0.19 x 9.21 inches
Language: eng

www.triestepublishing.com

You May Also Like

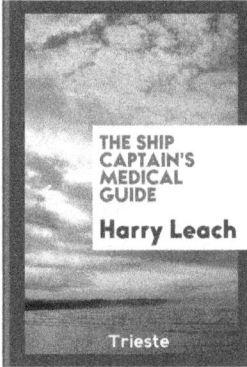

The Ship Captain's Medical Guide

Harry Leach

ISBN: 9781760570620
Paperback: 120 pages
Dimensions: 6.14 x 0.25 x 9.21 inches
Language: eng

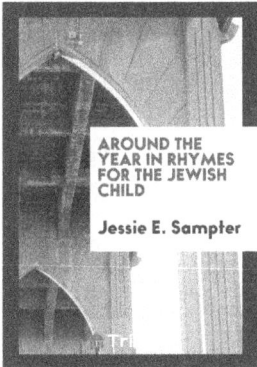

Around the Year in Rhymes for the Jewish Child

Jessie E. Sampter

ISBN: 9781760570712
Paperback: 104 pages
Dimensions: 5.83 x 0.22 x 8.27 inches
Language: eng

Find more of our titles on our website. We have a selection of thousands of titles that will interest you. Please visit

www.triestepublishing.com

CPSIA information can be obtained
at www.ICGtesting.com
Printed in the USA
LVHW04s1559240718
584775LV00012B/1039/P